I0568613

THE SEVEN-FIGURE MARKETING MINDSET FOR NOVELISTS

JODY J. SPERLING

CRE8 COLLABOR8 PRESS

ISBN: [978-1-959613-00-8]

Cover design by Ashley J.

Printed in the United States of America

cre8 collabor8 Press, 309 N. Thomas St. Oakland, NE 68045

Some names and identifying details of people described in this book have been altered to protect their privacy.

For Ash

THE SEVEN-FIGURE MARKETING MINDSET FOR NOVELISTS

Jody J. Sperling

Host of THE RELUCTANT BOOK MARKETER

THE ELEPHANT IN THE ROOM

This book will start where every book has ever started, with zero copies sold. But for you to have read these lines, some version of marketing must have occurred. Perhaps I personally asked you to buy the book. Or maybe by hard work and good fortune, a friend recommended the book to you, giving me the most precious of all sales, one by word of mouth.

Given the book's absurd title, you might be tempted to envision the emperor's new clothes. Who is this author who claims to have a seven-figure mindset to teach me but hasn't sold seven-figure's-worth of books?

It's a fair question, one we'll return to from other angles, and for now let's acknowledge I'm not claiming to know *how* to sell a million books or touch a million lives. Look to Stephen King or Danielle Steel for that. What I'm promising, and what you can learn from me because I've already done it, is to embrace an insatiable mindset that keeps you moving toward your outrageous goals with persistence, tenacity and resilient flexibility.

Pulling from my work as a real estate investor, I know how to act in the face of fear. I know how to overcome my own mind's objections when doubt creeps in. When you are tempted to retreat in fear, I can teach you a mindset that primes you to advance and with empowerment.

When I was a hundred thousand dollars in debt and everyone thought me a fool for getting into rental properties, I learned how to cultivate a mindset of abundance so strong naysayers could not deter me. And I can teach you to do the same.

Judge the book based on what it delivers. If you don't walk away enriched and brimming with confidence that you can achieve the goals you always dreamed of, if you don't finish this book with concrete tools for how to daily strengthen your mind against fear, uncertainty, and doubt, I want you to call me out publicly.

I invite you to rate this book so poorly no sane reader would ever touch it again, but if you do feel enriched, the same applies. Shout it from the mountain tops. Because if you win the game of mindset, you will achieve all your goals and more.

When you find the book delivers, just as I said it would, do me a favor, get it into a friend's hands. I'll thank you, and so will your friend.

BEFORE YOU START: UNDERSTAND OBJECTIVITY

If you've been writing for longer than a week and have ventured into the writing community you've heard somebody claim "good writing is subjective."

There's truth in that statement, but it's also used as a way to hide behind insecurity and uncertainty. Enjoyment may be subjective. Quality isn't.

Even if you're a rare person afflicted with geophagia—the compulsive desire to eat dirt—the quality of dirt matters. There's lead-filled dirt from urban housing lots and there's Amazonian, undisturbed earth. The first poisons you, the latter nourishes. Neither would qualify as a culinary delight.

The reason it's critical to start together here is that everything we discuss, every bit of mindset shift you accomplish, will be wasted if the objective quality of your writing falls short.

You can argue grammar is a tool of oppression to privilege the educated, and you can lament arcane rules created by stuffy old dead dudes that have no place in modern fiction, but you will find a book without sensible, grammatical logic will undermine every effort to earn an audience.

If you aren't committed to the use of proper grammar and

style in your novel writing, no amount of mindset adjustments will empower you to win a million readers. It is in your best interest to return this book, or better yet, gift it to someone who will commit to following the rules of the language since you will be unable to succeed without rules.

Let me, though, debunk one possible misconception that arises often when I discuss grammar.

You may write from the first-person perspective of an uneducated character, one who misspells words, uses unfamiliar sentence construction, and chooses unique methods of punctuating. As long as you create the rules of that character's writing and follow it as its own version of grammar, you'll have the same opportunity of success as those who follow textbook English.

Consistency, and service to the story are the two most important foundations to demand of your writing. If you are mindful of both, trust the process and you will write a great book.

We can't delight every reader. That's a big part of this book's purpose: I want to help you embrace a targeted audience. The mindset of selectivity primes us to selling the most copies of our books.

But before we seek our reader we have to know our book is a watertight vessel. If there are holes in it because the sentencing leads to reader confusion, the spelling ejects the reader from the immersive story, or the punctuation causes the reader to reread lines, potential raving fans will quit before you've won their trust and loyalty.

You'll work far too hard to allow your ideal reader an easy escape.

No mindset in the world can help a writer whose book is littered with technical mistakes to fight her way onto the New York Times Bestseller list. No level of determination can prep an author to read to a packed venue of fans if her writing technique earns her one-star reviews.

Before you read any further, ask yourself, "Is my book objectively ready for a reader?" You know it is if (1) you are confident in your understanding of the grammatical tools you used, (2) your trusted readers praise the story and pacing, (3) you've spent time and energy in multiple edits, proofreads, revisions, and rewrites, and (4) a third-party editor has okayed it for publication.

Please know, we all need third-party editors. None of us are above the misuse of homophones, and no matter how good spellcheckers have become it takes a slip of the fingers and "the" becomes "he" or "off" becomes "of".

From a technical aspect, the majority of writers have no clue how to outline and grope their way through many drafts to arrive at a coherent and pleasing story.

If you need help with grammar, it's not a sign you're a bad writer. But if you choose to publish a book with uneven writing and poor style choices, you are harming yourself. For the sake of your own dreams, don't shortcut the process, and stop claiming you can't afford to hire editors. Instead, realize you can't afford not to hire an editor.

Good writing is objectively good, even if the genre fails to appeal to every reader.

HOW TO READ
THIS BOOK

While some sections build upon each other, I've written this book so you can pick and choose which heading you want to read. Each heading addresses an anecdote, a self-contained mindset reflection, or a challenge to act.

There's no "right" way to read this book, but you will benefit most by moving slowly, and rereading seemingly simple sections.

My personal anecdotes are chosen with care to serve as a metaphor of a principle. I encourage you to reverse the instructive sections to relate them to stories in your own life. Doing so is how we provoke change in our mindsets and progress in our goals.

If you find benefit in this book, you'll enjoy my podcast, THE RELUCTANT BOOK MARKETER. Many of the section heading you read here have been explored from varying angles in episodes of my podcast, and most of the ideas have been refined and reworked into this book. You'll find the show anywhere pods are cast.

ABOUT THE AUTHOR

This is my first published book. I consider myself a novelist first and foremost. I've worked in sales and marketing since 2012. I have been a one-on-one coach for authors who want to improve their habits, writing style, and mindset, and my podcast, THE RELUCTANT BOOK MARKETER is in the top 3% of all podcasts.

I've learned directly from Forbes 500 CEOs, USA Today and New York Times bestselling authors, millionaire marketing experts, and trained mental health experts.

By talking with folks just like you who have bared their souls about the challenges and unexpected turns of marketing, I've learned a great deal about the mindset that leads to success.

I hold a Masters of Fine Arts with a Fiction focus from Eastern Washington University, and I contracted with a literary agent to represent my novel, *The Nine Lives of Marva DeLonghi.*

My choice to pursue traditional publishing for my fiction has kept me from putting out the numerous novels I've written over the past fifteen years, and it has afforded me the time to learn from traditional and self-published authors, how to shape the mindset to market for seven-figure success and beyond.

NOT EXACTLY A TRIGGER WARNING

If you picked up this book hoping to hear from an ethical teetotalling motivational author, that is one thing I cannot deliver. You may want to consider reading someone else. My rap sheet is measured in pages.

I'm a convicted arsonist, drunk driver, with an MIP. I was arrested for driving without a license, for lying to police officers, for theft, and public intoxication. Those are just the things I was caught doing.

And the reason I want you to know my past is because I want you to understand that whoever you are today, that person is in your past, but the tendencies that created that person still threaten your future. I still battle my impulses, and I still choose poorly.

If you continue reading, I hope you will be every bit as forgiving of yourself through this process of mindset adjustment as you are of me and my past. If you wary of a messy person, a work in progress, please know I do not begrudge you putting this book back in favor of something more suiting your needs. I'm interested in speaking to the ambitious, broken, often chaotic novelists who aren't ashamed to want seven-figure influence.

Some people want to tell the "I'm-reformed-you-can-trust-me-now-narrative."

I won't try that with you. I am reforming. It's an active process. I haven't stolen anything, for example, since the chocolate covered graham cracker at the Salt Lake City airport in 2015. I've been nicotine-free since 2020, but I still occasionally lose the battle to alcohol.

I had a day last weekend when I drank too much and some parts of that night are lost to the blackness. Truth is, I'm still a mystery to myself, and if you want somebody who's got it all figured out, I'm not your guide. But if you're okay learning from someone who stands after every fall, learns from every stumble, and loves to share from experience, let's change a million lives together with our books and our hearts.

CHAPTER ONE

THE BIRTH OF A MINDSET

DURING THE WINTER of 2021 I made a series of poor choices. I worked for a direct mail marketing company and the income I pulled was about a third what my income had been only months prior.

That's the life of anyone whose income has performance-based incentives or sales commission. We're familiar with the ramp-up period. And I want to take full responsibility for my failure, because I should've accepted it was my time to launch my own business, but I was afraid and so I blamed the company for my difficulties.

I decided that since they had withheld historic losses across the sales team I had the right to dissemble about my efforts.

I'd justified I'd been sold a false bill of goods. Every team member in my Midwest group separately told me they felt sorry for me inheriting the book of business I'd taken over. Not a good sign! And yet had I wanted to, I could have adjusted my level of effort such that I could have sold even in that most challenging of times.

See, I'd gone in with the wrong attitude to begin with. I told myself with a background in sales, having sold everything from sunglasses to workers compensation insurance, I could make the direct mail marketing a successful position with minimal effort.

But after three months with only two, minor new accounts to my name, I admitted to my wife I'd taken an ill-fitting job I sucked at and wasn't willing to get better doing. I tried soothing my wounded ego and my broken morality by telling myself at least I'd acted with the best of intentions.

I'd wanted autonomy, to work from home. After all, I'd left my insurance job after the CEO said all employees would be returning full-time to the office following the COVID-19 pandemic.

The problem was, during the pandemic, working for the insurance carrier, I'd managed to build a portfolio of rental houses. I owned four rentals, and had exceptional cash flow because of my equity position, but not enough to cover my bills.

I saw the distance yet to go to create enough income to have the sort of life I wanted. Perhaps if my family hadn't moved an hour outside of Omaha to buy our primary house, I'd have denied the voice inside me screaming to break out and risk it all.

Maybe I'd have returned to the office for another year, long enough to accumulate a couple more rentals and pad my income. But because I didn't want to work an eight-hour day and drive two hours while fitting in daily novel writing and reading, I decided to leave the insurer to gamble on the remote, direct marketing job.

During all of this, something scary had been happening, something insidious I failed to recognize until I had a moment of clarity. As with so much of life, clarity resulted from pain.

You might relate, but I've never been one for employment

in the first place. The more oversight I have, the worse I perform. Give me autonomy and ensure me if I accomplish the outlined objectives I'll be in good standing, and I am a machine of driving efficiency.

The reason is simple. I have passions outside employment. I want to be a full-time novelist. I want to write bestselling, prize-winning books. I'm never happier than when I'm reading and writing fiction.

Give me obligation-free, limitless time and I'll tend to fill the schedule with long blocks of writing and reading, alternating with short excursions to exercise—walking mostly. I'd gladly walk twelve miles daily.

Thinking I'd have the autonomy I craved with the marketing company, and knowing I had a strength to sell customers cold with innovative and comedic emails, I expected to meet my marketing objectives in half the time I was supposed to log.

I banked on giving the marketing company a focused thirty hours a week while performing at 125%. Ego? Probably. Ignorance? Absolutely. But instead, I found I was working in excess of forty-hour weeks and achieving roughly 10% of expectations. Not only did I fail to bring in new customers, but I failed to keep those who'd been clients when I started.

I'll accept blame. I didn't sell hard to existing customers once I heard the stories about their campaign failures. Rather than committing to fixing problems, I got angry. A great auto shop I liked hadn't gained a single new customer on a five-thousand dollar buy. I lacked the heart to ask for trust and had no desire to find outside-the-box solutions.

So around November of 2021, I decided I was going to let the marketing job go, but not without my revenge. Instead of quitting when I knew I was ready to leave, I decided I'd let the company pay me what I deemed they owed me before letting me leave.

I justified my choice to take salary for no meaningful work

because they had been dishonest about the prospects of the job when they hired me.

Thin excuse? Gaunt to say the least. Like I've stated twice: I justified horrifically. I wish I'd had the courage to quit and give the company an honest review because they were liars and frauds, but I got what I deserved.

For two months I worked around the clock recording my podcast, writing my novel, building my brand and preparing myself for life after employment. All the activity almost distracted me from my complete collapse of ethics. The only redeeming quality about me those two months was my dogged efforts and determination.

It all ended the week prior to Christmas. My boss called on a Monday morning to inform me he was placing me on a Performance Improvement Plan. Instead of going through the motions and prolonging my demise until I was fired, I said, "Sorry, pal. No can do."

That was my last day there.

PAIN AS A TEACHER AND MOTIVATOR

Let's rewind a bit to the pain and to the revelation.

My literary agent signed me in April 2019. At that time I was working for the insurance carrier and I recall writing the words "200k Jody" on a novelty chalkboard pinned to the wall of my cubicle.

My wife renamed me "200k Jody" in her iPhone attached to an embarrassing photo of me rubbed down in coconut oil flexing like Arnold Schwarzenegger. (I'd been sunburned badly earlier that day and was in damage-control mode.)

Anyway, we knew my agent was going to find a handful of editors who would fight over my manuscript, and the ensuing bidding war would result in a two hundred thousand dollar advance from the winning publishing house.

In June, when we finally went out on submission, I struggled to sleep. The expectations, the anticipation, the knowing crowded my mind at all times.

Then June slipped into July, turned into August, faded into September, blew into October, and melted into November. One by one every editor declined to offer.

My agent sent it out to more editors, but without results.

I remember the day I clocked in, looked at the novelty chalkboard on my cubicle wall, and decided to erase the words there, replacing them with a drawing of a cheeseburger. It turned out, the burger was more prophetic than the projected novel advance had been.

From December of 2020 until May of 2022, I gained consistent weight, ballooning from 185lbs. to 260lbs.

The physical deterioration should've been the only sign I needed to know what had happened to me, but I missed it because I was a convincing actor, even to myself. I still daily wrote and read. In fact, I read more books in 2020 than in 2019, more in 2021 than in 2020. I read close to 200 books in 2021.

How could someone that prolific be a quitter, a giver-upper?

But that is exactly what I was. I was a quitter. I'd given up on my dream of publishing.

And because I no longer believed my literary agent would find me a publisher, I decided to build a portfolio of rental houses as a form of passive income. This should've been a dead giveaway to anyone looking in from the outside. I even called my rental houses "patrons of the arts."

I bragged about them as being the patrons that supported my writing, all the while not knowing I'd replaced the roaring, burning passion to publish with a roaring burning passion to accumulate a large real estate portfolio.

Despite a driving depression that gripped me around the fall of 2020, I failed to connect my situation and circumstances to my outlook. Instead I studied psychedelics and their reported power at creating profound change when used therapeutically.

The pain of darkness, the hopelessness, it fueled a desperate search that led to an opportunity to use psilocybin in September of 2021. The experience defied explanation. Do I recommend everyone have this experience? No. Was it profound for me? Yes. Perhaps I'll write about it elsewhere, but the day was no magic bullet. In fact, it left me terrified and confused.

But following a two-week existential crisis of identity, one day while walking my dog, I envisioned a whole new life.

I saw a life in contrast to the life I'd been living. It matched me and suited my needs and made sense for my life and filled every gaping hole I'd been trying to nurse back to health.

First called cre8 collabor8, my business would be a publisher that found and interviewed aspiring novelists like me who'd sought publication but failed. I meant to give them an audience of listeners. The listeners would vote for their favorite story each season, and the winning story would be published by cre8 collabor8.

Needless to say, that idea flopped, but it did launch me into the journey that helped me do what I needed to do. It was then I backed away from trying to make the direct mail marketing work.

It was then I decided we'd sell our rental houses and use the profits from those to give us the income to support our family while I went full-time as an author and podcast host, building my brand, building my platform, living my dream.

REVELATION ISN'T SUCCESS & SUCCESS IS PERSONAL

Wouldn't it be nice if the story was a rocket launch of success from there? Man wrestles with self-deception, doubt, depression and fear, overcomes his demons and flies. This story is more like, man wrestles with all those dark feelings, and his demons use the unknown to prey on him during quiet moments.

It's true. I struggled with more pain as my podcast slowly dwindled from an opening month of roughly 400 downloads to a February of 250 downloads.

To put it in perspective for you, any podcast you can name has upwards of 10,000 downloads a month, and a podcast with 10,000 downloads a month earns only about $1,500 a month from ad revenue. Up until 5,000 downloads a month, a podcast must rely on products, services and affiliates for any income whatsoever.

It quickly became apparent I'd hurt myself by failing to brand on social media. My former belief that a good book would find readers proved almost fatal. I needed listeners, followers, fans, but finding them from scratch was a full-time job in itself.

Despite setbacks, foolishness, and what seemed a lack of support from all but my wife, I found each day, awaking was a gift, and I loved the journey. My writing, though pinched into smaller timeframes, was rich. My reading, though far less prolific, felt purposeful.

I thought about what had changed and realized where I'd failed. It helped that I had the ears and mouths of people on my podcast interviews who'd done what I wanted to do. The seven-figure marketing mindset for authors came from these moments.

It became the compass by which I travel, and in the months since I committed, amazing things have happened, things I have learned and can help you replicate, but whether you walk the journey like me or choose a different path to suit you, the mindset I adapted will help you.

More than practical tips, at the foundation of how-to practices, your mindset will ensure success. I can tell you from experience, when you act rightly, you'll move quickly upward. When you act wrongly, you'll stall, regress or hinder progress to a great degree. It's usually easy to tell how you're acting if you become good at accepting natural feedback from your surroundings.

But because we're stubborn, most of us will endure failure too long before pivoting. I want to teach you the mindset to not only endure as you battle your stubborn self-imposed limitations, but the mindset to recognize foolish action and correct it faster. That is the seven-figure marketing mindset for novelists.

IS THE 7-FIGURE MARKETING MINDSET THE ONLY WAY?

Many authors will confess to a dream of earning a living on their writing. They hope one of their books will be a breakout success and afford them the freedom to embrace full-time self-employment, but few authors maintain mental and emotional momentum after a few setbacks.

While it's true some authors do nothing to market themselves and still find great success, most authors have to labor with single-minded focus to experience the kind of breakthrough that leads to the full-time writing lifestyle.

I know an author who has no social media, writes only when inspiration strikes, and yet published the first of two novels she sold to Viking.

Two of her short stories were optioned by a major Hollywood director. She is a stay-at-home mother. She'll be the first to admit her luck as astounding.

If you want to leave your future as an author to luck, follow her path. If you'd rather follow a guaranteed path to success, broad readership, and generational wealth, read this book until the mindset and accompanying action feels so familiar it's like brushing your teeth.

WHY NOT SIX-FIGURE OR EIGHT-FIGURE MARKETING MINDSET?

This book is titled the SEVEN-FIGURE MARKETING MINDSET because I'm not yet courageous enough to call it the billionaire handbook for novelists' domination.

A million of something still stretches me. Though I want to, I struggle to think in larger numbers yet. Touching nine million lives seems so vast, yet it's a number I can visualize.

But perhaps we can take comfort together in knowing the same mindset driving your journey to a million dollars and a million books sold is the mindset that will take you as far as you want to go. You may have heard it before, but look to almost any successful entrepreneur, and you won't have a hard time getting them to agree: the first million is the hardest.

Once you know how to scale, eight-, nine- or ten-figures is a factor of time, tenacity, and desire.

THE TIME-TESTED, MONEY-BACK GUARANTEE

You're going to read one phrase more than any other throughout this book: Action creates mindset.

Thinking the right thoughts means nothing if we don't act on the thoughts we think. Ever thought *I'd sure like to lose some weight*? How often do you act on that thought? Your waistline will tell the story.

If you act on a thought, results are guaranteed. Things like diet and exercise work. You will lose weight, but listen, we both know, especially when it comes to diet, the body itself fights back. We have enough quality research to know, at a cellular level, your body fights your mind to return it to its "set point".

Now, I'm not a doctor, but with a bit of nuance removed, I can tell you that any fat you pack on to your body will create a new "set point". That set point is where your physiological equilibrium anchors. If you go below the set point, the body sends chemicals to the nervous system asking to gain the fat back.

The further you go below the set point, the more tenacious the chemical bath to drag you back. You've experienced something else like this before. The further the winter chill sinks below your thermostat's set point, the harder the thermostat runs to keep the house heated, and the more air your house bleeds to the outdoors.

Good news is, research has found ways to increase the efficiency of home insulation and research has found ways to reset your body's weight set points. While this isn't a book on health or homebuilding, what scientists have seen with body weight and thermal efficiency is great news for writers like us.

If you haven't noticed, I'm a big fan of metaphors, because I believe they have the power to create lasting change in how we view the world around us and ourselves. Health has played an important part in my life. Researching it is one of my favorite hobbies.

I challenge you, as you read to stretch my metaphors, to apply your own, to find connections from your life that help deepen your understanding. Nothing improves learning as much as taking what we learn and applying it to novel concepts we've already mastered.

If you do that, if you read this book, take action on the mindset exercises, and continue to fail at marketing your books, I'll buy a hundred copies of your novel and return you the price of my book. That's how confident I am in what this book can do for you.

What that means for you though is embracing a new mindset and acting to see it fulfilled. There will be truckloads of discomfort. You aren't going to achieve radical dreams with half-hearted changes.

CHAPTER
TWO

YOU ARE A SPECIFIC KIND OF WRITER

WHEN YOU CONSIDER what it means to succeed, you envision an international book tour with assistants planning your travel, booking your hotels, scheduling reading venues, and researching all the best stops along the way.

When you step on stage, the audience forgets the golf clap and roars with enthusiasm. You deliver your reading with humor, wit, and passion. Ninety-one percent of the people in the crowd buy your book and wait hours in line for a selfie and a signature.

You have this dream, and even though you've been quoted claiming you'd be happy if your books sold enough copies to support your financial responsibilities, you know that's only the beginning, a stepping stone on the way to worldwide bestseller, and subject of an eight-part biopic on Netflix. Step aside Ernest Hemingway; look out Shakespeare!

The world has taught you to be "reasonable" to be "polite" to be "patient", but if you want the kind of success you dream of, it's time to step into the ludicrous. It's time to discard modesty. It's time to embrace unreasonable demands on yourself. It's time for truth. It's time for mindset. It's time for action. Action creates mindset, and mindset enables action.

You can live your dream if you are willing to do what it takes, but understand, action is rare, and most people are happy to stop at fantasies, living the dream rather than acting in a way that can make your goals a reality. Be honest with yourself. Do you want to impact a million readers, to sell a million copies of your books?

SELF-DECEPTION WILL NOT FOOL ANYBODY

As of today, you've written a handful of words, several you believe in. You've published but sales hardly trickle in. Perhaps you sell six copies a month, maybe fewer. You've dabbled in ads and you post about your book on social media, but it's like those posts are invisible, because no one engages.

You manage to get plenty of chatter when you post pictures of your dog or your children, but the moment you mention your book, you might as well toss it in the trash for all the conversation it starts. That discourages you, but you don't know how to fix the problem.

On the one or two occasions you've asked someone if they'd accept a free copy of your book for a fair and honest review, you've waited weeks to see the review pop up and received only crickets in reply. You grow resentful, but you're ashamed at your resentment because you know you haven't done what is required to attract a meaningful readership.

Driven to frustration, you've messaged a few people you think can perhaps help you, but the advice they give is just like the others. You've tried it, and it hasn't worked.

So you tell yourself, *I write for the pleasure of creating stories. It doesn't matter if I have a million readers. It only matters that I do my best*. But those words, *my best* sting because you know you could do better.

Meanwhile, you see the stories of authors whose second novel lands on the New York Times Bestseller list and all they can seem to do is act surprised like luck propelled them to such rarified air.

TAKING RESPONSIBILITY ONLY GOES SO FAR

In the 1960s the idea of a low-fat diet began to spread. It was touted as an optimal way for all people to live. By the 1980s a full-fledged low-fat and fat free culture had developed.

People were told to eat fat free diets to remain healthy, yet the incidents of obesity surged more than ever. As more information emerged, the perils of low-fat diets surfaced.

Rather than helping maintain a thin body, healthy blood pressure, low cholesterol and manageable hunger, low fat diets had promoted the opposite. The body was meant to ingest robust amounts of fats for optimal health.

Exactly opposite of the diet trends for twenty years, low fat promoted poor health while high fat diets with low carbohydrates were beneficial.

But for the millions of people who dutifully kept their fat intake low during this time period, learning that they'd been sabotaging their own health must've felt like a terrible betrayal, which is why many of us are reluctant to look at our situations with marketing our books.

It's difficult to accept you've been betraying your own best interests in favor of faulty trends and advice that has been at the center of the marketing-for-writer's conversation for decades. If you can accept you've been misled and determine to reorient your efforts, today can be the day you change from single-digit monthly sales to four-figure monthly sales and beyond.

Are you ready to act? Action creates mindset: Your first

task is to post on your favorite social media: "Do you know the name of my forthcoming novel?" Doing this will quickly show you how obscure you are and how much effort it will take to turn that problem around.

THE "DOING YOUR BEST" MYTH

What is your definition of "doing your best"? It can be a sensitive subject.

One person's best effort may be another person's baseline expectation for waking. And while I know you aren't the kind of person who struggles to get out of bed every day, because you wouldn't have opted to read a book titled *The Seven-figure Marketing Mindset for Novelists* if you were, you might still have high highs and low lows, radical swings in desire. (Here's a secret: so do I.)

I personally can't figure out Mondays. In December of 2021 I left my marketing job and with it, I thought I'd say goodbye to Monday. Though I work hard and put diligent effort into my writing, reading and podcast, Monday has long been a day of dread for me.

It may be a psychological hang-up, something with practice I could overcome, but so far, I'm not winning the battle against Monday. I cut back on indulgence on the weekend to help with neurochemicals, but that didn't help. I tried earlier bedtime on Sunday evening to no effect. I've experimented with varying fasting schedules. The problem persists.

I can say whatever I want, doing my best isn't overcoming my Monday blues. If you're anything like me, you might have your own version of Monday blues. Perhaps yours is an inclination to scrolling Instagram reels. Maybe you binge Hulu. You might be a gamer who gets lost on hours-long twitch campaigns and loses track of time.

But in the moments when we tangle with our Mondays,

we're far from doing our best. Does that mean we're bound to fail at accomplishing our seven-figure goals?

Instead of bound to fail, we're poised to succeed. How could that be? Because the places where we're powerless are the places where we gain the best information, have the most opportunity, and get the quickest feedback.

In my search to redeem Mondays, I discovered a missed opportunity. It came through reflection. Prior to leaving my employer to be my own boss, I found that I had actually begun to look forward to Mondays for a short period of time. So what had I done differently during those months? By examining what changed, I recognized something I'd sacrificed that mattered to me.

When I had an employer, Mondays meant a return to routine, to quiet, and to open time for research. Judge any way you want, but when I clocked in to sell insurance or direct mail ads on Monday, the first two hours of the day were spent catching up on matters I cared about.

I'd see what new fasting videos were out, what new books my favorite authors were working on, what podcast episodes I needed to binge, and what real estate investing news I could read. I scrolled the latest Cubs rumors and even browsed Marvel comics' updates. It was a mix of entertainment, research, and inspiration that got me excited for the week.

But once I created an LLC and I was racing against the clock to get my podcast and writing monetized—I hate the word monetized, and I'm starting to hate what it means—I felt I had to cut that time out of my calendar. I needed to earn a living to support myself, my three sons and Ashley, and I wanted to feel both useful and invulnerable.

Because I'd convinced myself every hour counted toward this goal—and in real ways every hour *does* count—I sacrificed that leisurely flow into Monday mornings. The result though, was a dread that could cause the entire day to be a struggle.

By trying to sacrifice Monday mornings to monetization, I'd lost the whole day to dread and dislike. So I gave myself Monday mornings back, and now that research has become part of my podcast planning.

Whatever my flavor of the month is, whatever I'm most excited to binge on, whether it's developments in healthful eating, the newest Captain America rumors, or a forthcoming Stephen King novel, I incorporate the stories I'm most excited to devour as metaphors into my podcasts.

Your Monday won't have the same recipe mine does, but I'm guessing that behind whatever your Monday is, you'll find something critical to your flourishing that you're with-holding because you believe it's a weakness.

I encourage you to go all-in on whatever gives you energy. Whether it's gaming, viewing, climbing, any other -ing you're into, go all in and sacrifice your Monday morning to it. (And listen, your Monday morning might be on a Thursday evening. It's not about the time, it's about the moment. I give you permission to take back your guilty plea-sure. Embrace it.

Perhaps you think Netflix reveals your laziness. Maybe you think gaming shows your failure of imagination. You might even believe Instagram is bad for you in any amounts.

What if, instead, you could find ways to use the things you're turning to for escape into something influential in your creative life. What would happen to your relationship with your guilty pleasure if you turned it into your intentional inspiration?

Imagine scheduling a few hours once a week to scroll reels on Instagram, but instead of feeling bad, you keep a notepad or writing device nearby, and you note what reels made you laugh, jump, or in general thrill? Could you inspect what about those reels worked and bring it back to your writing to improve the craft?

You have a favorite Netflix show. Maybe you open a voice

memo on your phone and speak a few notes about the story that most impacted you, where it failed, where it soared.

If you game, what keeps you hooked into a level or campaign? Take notes. In each case, you're imitating the process I discovered with my Monday mornings, and not only are you redeeming that time you used to give away mindlessly, but you're teaching yourself to engage with the things you sought escape in in ways that enrich the activity.

Sometimes strict boundaries are part of the equation. My Mondays can still derail if I drink too much alcohol on a Sunday. And even with my playful research restored, I need to give myself vigorous exercise on Monday mornings in the form of burpees. Getting the blood flowing helps.

But all of this is the mindset activity that preps me to have success the remainder of the day and throughout the week. Abstinence, you may find is overrated, and in all likelihood, unnecessary. Get your mindset toward obstacles right, take aligned action, and see if you don't notice profound and immediate changes toward the things you thought irre-deemable.

FINDING YOUR STORY

I began my podcast, formerly titled cre8 collabor8, with the goal of hosting a competition for aspiring writers to publish their books. I intended to hire an editor and a marketer as the platform grew. But I had no clue how challenging that goal would be.

Furthermore, I began to see all the ways operating that business would drain me. My dream is to share my work with the world, but I had no clue how to reach the people in my own town, much less my state, not to mention the whole world!

That said, as I groped for what I wanted to do, what would give purpose to talents, I discovered I had something few writers did, a natural inclination toward selling and marketing.

It's been true of me since forever: when I have a product I'm passionate to sell, the hidden, gregarious side of me emerges. My fear of strangers dissipates. Endless energy to communicate with other emerges. I speculate you're the same. That's the thing. You might label yourself introverted, but how much of that has to do with not connecting to something you care about?

I realized I had a lot to say about marketing a book. Not only that, but the things I had to say helped people think in new ways about their marketing, helped them shift focus away from confusion and despair toward optimism and determination.

That led me to rebranding cre8 collabor8 into THE RELUCTANT BOOK MARKETER. The reluctance has two meanings. It's my own reluctance to embrace this marketing journey for the first three years of having a literary agent, but it's also a signal to all the novelists out there who want to sell their books but hesitate to learn marketing.

My podcast, this company, exists to tell novelists marketing can be fun and fruitful if you focus on abundance and impact. Your mindset makes all the difference.

Your story is going to be different than mine, but if you examine where you've been and take the time to consider your own history, the contribution you have to make will be evident.

Use the part of yourself that naturally emerges when you're excited about whatever you have passion for to market your books. It will be a unique force of energy that propels you forward.

THE DIFFERENCE BETWEEN HOW & HOW-TO

There are plenty of books out there that deal with the who, what, where, why, when, and how of marketing. Men like Russell Brunson and Pat Flynn have achieved seven-figure status in more ways than one. They're millionaires in the bank and in their followings.

Pat and Russell have built their platforms teaching funnels and providing guides, but their focus often neglects how the small business impacts our mind.

A funnel is no good if you don't enjoy building it. The mindset you approach your journey with creates the foundation for your success, and if you want to move from "trying and failing" to "doing and succeeding," you have to reframe your mindset.

Though, if you think all the work of mindset can be done from a comfy chair, you've got a bit of a shock coming. Mindset, as I've said, follows action, and if you're 100% committed to developing the seven-figure marketing mindset to sell your novel, you'll have to act in ways that will remain uncomfortable.

ACTION STARTS CLOSE TO HOME

In 2020, I had an opportunity to buy a house I knew was a stellar deal. It was in a great neighborhood, needed light repairs and was listed far below market value. I called my real estate agent and asked him to offer on the property.

We lost the bid by **$1000**.

If I'd trusted my instincts, I would've had that house and made an instant six-figure gain in equity, because I knew what my agent neglected to consider. There was a fourth bedroom with an egress window already installed in the basement, but it wasn't considered a room in the pricing because it had only been framed and not drywalled.

A few days of easy labor would've changed that.

I lost an opportunity to make two year's salary in one day, because I didn't assert myself. If I could have that moment back, I'd do it very differently. Don't trust anyone who tells you they have no regrets in life. If you have no regrets, you've never put yourself in a position to take big enough risks.

So what stopped me in the moment from ensuring I offered the winning bid? I'd chosen to listen to people's first comments without asking follow up questions.

A few friends were especially critical and insinuated I'd soon be living on the street if I took so much debt on. Where I could have asked if they understood the difference between unbacked debt and cash flowing debt, instead I resented their sense that I wasn't smart enough to grow my wealth.

I let their words slow me enough that I did what they suggested and entered a maximum bid for a conservative cost, an atypical posture for a usually assertive buyer. Unfortunately, regardless of what my agent thought, he accepted my plan without comment and we lost.

Fear kept me back, and I let the property go.

If you're looking to your friends and family for advice during times of stress, during moments of confronting the unknown, take everything with a smidge of skepticism and a mindset of curiosity plus determination. You can learn from feedback anywhere, but if you trust feedback when someone says no—and friends and family say no daily—if you trust feedback without questioning the point of view from which it's given, I guarantee you'll make the same poor decisions I did.

Let me remind you again. I missed out on six-figure profits because of my cowardice.

RESPONDING TO CRITICISM FROM FRIENDS & FAMILY

The majority of writers have been trained to approach this conundrum in one of two ways: Either they say, "I don't share my work with family and friends so they can't criticize me," or they say, "I shrug it off and move on, because they aren't my target audience."

If you find yourself responding in either of those ways, you are sacrificing opportunities for personal and professional success. You're committing to failure.

It is true: Your family and friends are most likely not your target audience, and knowing that puts you at an advantage over those who believe their family owes it to them to buy a copy of their book. However, when a family member responds critically to your writing dreams, you have an opportunity.

Just like I could've learned more about the mindset of my friends when I had the opportunity to buy that house at a discount, a mindset that would've helped me take bold action instead of retreating, you can take bold action too.

When your family says, "Your book is too vulgar, no one will read it," you can feel resentment and secretly brood that they are puritanical, or you can ask, "When you say too vulgar, who is it too vulgar for?" They might follow up with a simple reply such as, "It's too vulgar for me," and you can then ask, "I respect that. Do you think any of your friends would read it?"

Something unexpected might happen here. Your family member might say, "Connie reads vulgar trash all the time. I mean, every time I see her she's talking about some foul-mouthed detective in one of her silly books."

All of a sudden, you went from feeling vaguely shameful for being an author who wrote vulgar trash to having a solid lead on someone who might read and love your book. And chances are, Connie is friends with other mystery readers who can't get enough vulgar trash to satisfy their reading habits.

You suddenly not only have a potential reader, but you have a refill of confidence that there are people out there who do appreciate what you're doing. It's a mindset win you caused to happen by acting boldly where you could have retreated.

But what if it's more passive aggression? Say you call your father to catch up on his life and he asks you when you're going to get a real job. Instead of feeling hurt again, what if you ask what a real job is and listen without offense, even ask what it would look like for your writing to be considered a real job.

Maybe he'll tell you how 90% of startups never turn profitable and that 10% shutter their doors within the first twelve months and another 80% can't outlast five years.

Would that open the door for you to reframe your situation to him? What if you've already been writing for a decade with a handful of print publications, journals, magazines, and newspapers. Perhaps you show him how responsibly you've built toward your writing career.

It may be that the healthiest and most productive route is to distance from family and unsupportive friends, but in many cases, well-considered questions and reasoned answers with follow-up questions lead to insight and a shift in support.

It's not for our family or our friends that we ask these questions and work to shift their mindset. We're acting on our behalf, and we will fail at times when we're in the moment. Though, with each conversation we grow in our understanding of what it looks like to write with purpose and an entrepreneurial mindset. Act even if you aren't ready. It's the only way forward.

It may be a while yet before you're cashing checks from your writing, but you have a stellar opportunity to practice a focused mindset today that will set you up to have seven-figure success in your marketing when publication day arrives.

REJECTIONS ALL THE WAY DOWN

In the spring of 2013 I began sending applications to MFA graduate programs. I'd followed the conventional wisdom of picking dream schools, stretch schools, realistic schools, and safety schools in my application process.

Of the ten applications I submitted, three accepted my application, but none offered me assistance. One program was on my safety list. The other two were on my realistic school list.

And listen, nothing against Eastern Washington University. Spokane is still among my favorite places in the world. It's got a small-town vibe with enough culture to appeal to a big city soul.

But when you live in a town of 900 residents and you have a 6-month-old son with severe colic and you've already been pining after a publishing deal with FSG for the better part of ten years landing at a realistic school as a barely accepted student, it stings a little.

And let me offer a little more context. Ashley and I had been enjoying one of our long walks in downtown Omaha on a date during the building-a-list phase of the application process. At the time, if I haven't already mentioned it, we were fervent church-going protestants.

Did I mention our walk was a prayer walk? We were trendy Christian sorts who brought mugs of Arabica coffee with us and reached out to the Lord for guidance, and this was one of those walks. As we were praying, Ashley had a vision of gold and navy.

She knew I needed to apply to the University of Michigan. At that time, I had no idea about the quality of the

Michigan MFA program. My eyes and dreams were firmly set on the Iowa Writers' Workshop. Flannery O'Connor had graduated the program and Marilynne Robinson taught there. It was my number one reach school.

Turns out, Michigan was ranked number two, just behind Iowa in the polls in 2013.

So with God's blessing I bumped off Columbia as a reach school and applied to Michigan instead. It was an easy choice. When the God of the universe commissions something, you tend to move with a little swagger in your step.

I've spoiled how this whole thing ends, but you already knew that. Counting on gods to give us what we want is the wrong mindset, and that counts no matter what religion you follow as you read this book, because you can't find anywhere in your religious text where you're promised a path to the top of the mountain.

Using your legs or wheelchair or hand-operated mobility-device is still the only proven way to climb anything.

But where were we? I was positive Michigan would accept my application, and not just that but, with a full-ride scholarship. So as the final semester of my undergraduate studies wound down, I would drive the hour commute from my school to my small-town house dreaming of the reveal.

The reveal?

Yeah, it's embarrassing. But it takes a little context to understand the mental contortions I performed to have this specific fantasy.

See, I'd given Ashley all the passwords to my accounts because that's what honest and open husbands do. Don't question it. And because she had all my passwords, she looked at my email and such when the mood struck.

We had an agreement. If she looked at my email, she had to star anything she'd readS so I understood she'd seen it, but I hadn't. It was a clever system...clever.........

I, though, believed throughout the application process that

when the acceptance email from Michigan came, she would find it first and file it to surprise me with later. Or maybe they'd send a letter through the mail only.

Either way. The point was, she'd get to the good news before me, and she'd plan a surprise to give the moment even more delicious weight: "Hey, baby, do you know what the temperature in Ann Arbor is today? Hint, hint...It's hot!!!"

On the return commute from Omaha, the final turn was a left off Highway 77 onto 2nd Street. The Lutheran church with its beige stucco walls and silver steeple obscured my house, second on the next north/south block, Davis Avenue.

There was a moment before I reached the alley behind Davis that I could see the porch and bay window of our house. Each day, returning from school, my heart would quicken in anticipation of that moment because I'd convinced myself Ashley would have bought and hung a Michigan University, navy and gold flag, from the window, confirming our destiny.

Instead, on a sunny day more summerlike than springish, a flimsy envelope with the Michigan logo in the upper left-hand corner arrived at my house. I knew by its weight what message it contained. Ashley and I cried together. I spent an evening on our front porch smoking cigarettes and drinking beer.

When I later accepted the invite from Eastern Washington University, I did so as the biggest loser in Nebraska.

RESPONDING TO REJECTION

Most writers respond to this obstacle by either saying, "Rejection is part of life. Have thick skin," or, "Everyone gets rejected. Writing is a subjective business."

You probably already guessed, but if you subscribe to either of these responses you've already signed your surrender. It's time to reevaluate your mindset on rejection so it can lead to acceptance and lasting success.

Rather than dismissing rejection as part of the process, use every opportunity of being rejected as one to question the status. Let me caution you, if you try the following technique, it may destroy your reputation if you submitted your work or application with inferior materials.

Consider that if you failed to follow submission guidelines, if you submitted work that was half-baked, if you ignored clear prompts, drawing attention to yourself will have catastrophic consequences. Don't do that. Make every submission perfect if you want to challenge the status.

I THINK THERE'S BEEN A MISTAKE

My friend, we'll call him Bill, submitted a short story to a prestigious publication. one of those ones where all of the who's-who in fiction have published.

Bill sent in his best story. Six months later, he received the email notifying him that while such decisions are subjective, his work had been declined for publication.

Instead of tacking the rejection to the wall, Bill stared at his laptop screen for hours, dazed, offended, frustrated. Six months? for a form rejection? He felt indignant.

To hear Bill tell the story is to question how sincerely he believed what he said when he said, "I think there's been a mistake." According to his story now, he always felt the rejection had been mistakenly emailed to him and not another poor shmuck with a similar name.

But in the hours following his catatonic frustration, Bill called me to ask about a plan he'd had. The idea was, he'd find a phone number for the publication, call in and tell whoever picked up the phone there'd been a mistake.

Bill was convinced he'd negotiate his way into publication. No matter how much I tried to reason with him, he couldn't be persuaded to let the rejection go and move forward.

No amount of trying to help him graciously accept defeat could break through his determination, and the funny thing is, after a week of silence from Bill I got a midnight phone call. "You're not going to believe this!"

I glanced at Ashley and shrugged. "The rejection wasn't a mistake after all."

"Wrong! Dead wrong, bro."

I squinted at the TV, playing an episode of BREAKING BAD, and muted so I could take this call. Our son was finally drifting off after a long colicky night of screaming. "Excuse me?"

"They're publishing my piece, dude."

"I'm pretty tired and I must've misheard you." I knuckled my left eye. "I thought you said _____ is publishing your story."

"Yeah, man. They are."

I was struck dumb. Perhaps I congratulated him, but as the moment washed over me, I was struck by his stupid luck and a wave of feeling sorry for me. How did supernatural events of good luck happen to everyone but me?

There may have been some more discussion, but time has taken it all from me, all that is, but a lesson I spent too long learning.

STOP BEING GRACIOUS IN DEFEAT

Bill's phone call to the prestigious publication took guts. Most people couldn't convince themselves to try. Of those who could, many would fail to find a working phone number to dial. For those who got a phone number perhaps only one would suggest that the mistake had been made and mean it.

Because Bill knew his story was great, he sold out getting his point across. Maybe he caught an editor at the exact moment the editor was feeling generous. Regardless, the outcome allowed Bill an opportunity to share real estate with the industry's top talent, and today, Bill is in the midst of writing his second novel of a two-book deal as a Penguin Random House author.

Had he taken my advice and been gracious in defeat, his books would not be on shelves across the country today.

Now, do I think I should've followed up with the University of Michigan. Would that sort of brute-headed force work for anyone? No. As I said, if your submission isn't perfect, you'll get a reputation as a pain in the ass—pardon the language—and no one will work with you.

There are authors out there who have queried every agent on Querytracker.com but haven't had so much as a form rejection in years. It's not by mistake that they hear nothing back. Long ago, agents shared across agencies about these mass-querying authors and the email address was added to the spam list.

If you aren't tactful with your refusal to accept rejection, you'll be spammed for life. So understand, refusing to accept rejection is a high risk play, but it's at the heart of every successful writer's career.

And, sure, your story might not be Bill's. Author's like Stephen King refused to accept rejection by sending story after story after story to magazines. He wrote novel after novel in pursuit of greatness.

But like Bill, King knew his work had the spark of inevitability. Had you spoken to him before Carrie was accepted he'd never have said, "Publishing takes luck," or "The industry is rigged," or, "Maybe it's just not for me."

The next time you receive a rejection, consider it from the new mindset astounded by defeat. What can you do to change that no into a career-defining yes?

THE STORY OF A PODCAST

I launched THE RELUCTANT BOOK MARKETER in January of 2022. My first day, I just missed 100 downloads. It took north of six months before I broke the 100 downloads a day mark. Now I nearly double that number almost daily.

Between launch day and my first 100 download day, I saw more instances of 1-per-day and 2-per-day than I'd care to admit. I endured moments of agonizing self-doubt so fierce I dreaded getting out of bed in the mornings.

During that time, my primary solution to gaining downloads was to post about my podcast on Facebook. Looking back, I'm not sure why I thought posting on Facebook would achieve anything, but my mind told me the objective was to get my preestablished friend circle to become fans of my work.

I think I believed—again why, I don't know—that my friends would become raving fans and evangelize about my podcast on my behalf.

The laugh in all this is I'm far from alone in using that strategy. This isn't about statistics, but realize the majority of podcasts stop airing before completing forty episodes. There is even a term now for this outcome. It's called podfade.

For the month of January, my podcast brought in 401 downloads. In February that total was halved. By the last week of February I knew I had to act unreasonably so I spent, what for me, was an ungodly sum of money to join a mastermind for podcasters.

In the way that is characteristic of me, when I realized the expensive course would no suddenly alter the trajectory of my reach, I became bitter and blamed the man who had sold me, calling him a swindler and charlatan.

And in the way that is also characteristic of me, I poured over the course, attended every meeting offered, and redoubled my efforts. From that, I created a handful of valued relationships and one of the group members, we'll call him Jeff, shared with me that he had had more success growing his podcast through Twitter than on any other social media. Talk about a lightbulb moment.

Now, the Matrix-Neo-eating-a-cookie-and-breaking-a-plate dilemma (don't worry if you aren't following, but do go watch the original Matrix as it will blow your mind) for me is, would I have met Jeff if I hadn't spent the ungodly sum?

I'm guessing not, because the money forced me to find the value. What happened, and you'll hear this story over and over again, is that my investment in the podcast, financial commitment to it, created an appropriate level of desperation.

I wasn't about to be a fool.

This had to work because otherwise I just flushed some serious coin down the toilet. So I pressed into every drop of content the mastermind organizer had to offer and began to build relationships with writers who could benefit from what my podcast had to teach.

The book you're holding in your hands is the culmination of the lesson I learned: make people pay out of their wallet, because financial investments drive motivation, but give away uncommon value because goodness should be affordable to every budget.

THE STORY OF A PODCAST VIEWED FROM ANOTHER ANGLE

If you learned about this book from my podcast, you know the podcast is free. If you love what I'm doing, you've probably told at least one friend about my show. And, if you love my guests and buy their books after listening to an interview, a portion of the book profits comes to me through affiliate links.

I also have affiliate relationships with Social Dog[1], the finest Twitter management tool ever created, and I have an affiliate deal with Xero Shoes[2], the only brand of shoes you should be wearing if walking, running, writing, or jumping is important to you.

As my podcast grows, I'll accumulate more affiliate relationships, and one day soon I'll have sponsors run ads on my show. These tools allow me to give away all of my knowledge free of charge. Truth is, you won't find anything in this book I haven't spoken at length about in my podcast.

What you will find in this book is a coherent collection of a mindset reduced to its most valuable components for quickest digestion and repeated exposure.

I'll never be able to tell you how much of my podcast's success, rising from an unranked show to one receiving more downloads monthly than 97% of all podcasts, has to do with the mastermind I joined and how much has to do with the money I spent, and how much has to do with the mindset I cultivated.

What I can tell you, without reservation, is that I regret none of my decisions to leave my W-2 in December, or a dollar I've spent on my personal development.

I firmly believe there are masterminds out there now that offer stellar value to their members, and it is likely I'll enroll in another at some future time. This is an important point you need to understand. I use the word need sparingly for a reason, and I choose it here because it can be the fulcrum for your success.

The seven-figure marketing mindset depends on your willingness to invest time, money, energy, and obstinance in yourself and your book. You can't get there for free. Action creates mindset. You're responsible to act for your success by investing your money on it.

CHAPTER
THREE

WHAT WE SAY MATTERS

THE MAJORITY of people will look at their feet and in a barely audible voice say, "I don't know," or, "I've tried everything and nothing's worked," or, "Keep trying, results are bound to come sooner or later."

Let's examine each of these comments. We'll start with "I don't know." On its face, admitting a lack of knowledge is empowering, but the way we approach our limitations matters.

Instead of "I don't know," try saying, "I'm still searching." This small shift in wording has big implications. You've gone from being a passive observer to an active participant.

"I've tried everything, and nothing's worked," seems like the quitter's mentality, but like not knowing, it's only a subtle shift from being a productive admission. See what happens when you add a couple words: "I've tried everything *I know*, and nothing's worked *yet*." You have a powerful self-affirmation and a clear objective.

If you've tried everything *you know* and nothing's worked

yet, you're one resource away from a major breakthrough, and suddenly all you have to do is spend some time educating yourself with things like THE RELUCTANT BOOK MARKETER podcast, or Becky Robinson's BOOK MARKETING ACTION PODCAST.

THE PLAYING FIELD MATTERS

Every professional athlete dreams of playing on the largest stage. As a Chicago Cubs fan, I know the Major League system well. There are numerous developmental teams supporting the Big League club from rookie ball on up to Triple A.

As novelists, we often neglect to relate the outside world to our own situations, assuming no connections, but we can learn a great deal from the professional sports models.

If you haven't yet published a book, or if you have one on the market that's suffered low sales, don't act like you're in the Big Leagues. Everyone wrestles in the developmental leagues. Some authors race through. Others never see the packed stadium.

If you want to race through the levels, you have to do what others are unwilling to do.

My friend and fantasy author J.V. Hilliard[3] is a great example of a writer who embraced the developmental system and has used it to build a growing brand that's earning a decent income for him each month.

Knowing Terry Gross won't be calling him any time soon, J.V. has partnered with a publicist who helps him book podcast guesting opportunities, local radio broadcasts, and even television gigs, but he hasn't left all booking in the publicist's court.

J.V. spent months developing relationships with rural libraries near his home town of Pittsburgh. Through those relationships he's gained earned media opportunities to give live, public readings from his book to audiences who are inclined to see new authors.

He describes his method as being a big fish in a small pond. In small towns people have fewer events to attend so they're more likely to come see an author read. It's not a packed house. Sometimes it's two people, but he sells books, hones his public persona, and cultivates his speaking resume.

You can reach rural communities surrounding your home in the same way. It's a low-risk, moderate-reward environment that can lead to larger opportunities as you develop your speaking and grow your backlist.

Without the key mindset engagement, authors would never see the opportunity in small towns. Without acting on what you know, you're banking on luck and nothing more. Best practice would be to put this book down and go make a list of small communities within an hour of your home. You can start building relationships with the libraries in those communities now.

THE LIE OF PERSEVERANCE

Likely the most insidious of the marketing mentalities is perseverance. Perseverance sounds so good on the surface. Keep trying, what can be wrong with that? Unfortunately, blind perseverance kills.

The problem with blind perseverance is what it ignores. And you should be wary of those who boast about perseverance unless they have a proven track record of successes behind them. When 90% of startups fail within five years, prevailing wisdom needs examining.

I have children. My children loved FINDING NEMO. It's a story of blind perseverance. A famous quote from those movies is spoken by Ellen DeGeneres's character, Dory: "Just keep swimming."

But without a lot of what my grandfather would call stupid blind luck and a helpful collaboration from other fish, continued swimming would've led to death. Perhaps, maybe, possibly, Disney omitted some more important contextual lessons, but let's hope you aren't taking all your cues from movies...

If we don't daily take inventory, searching for weak points, and if we fail to adjust, we won't progress. Anyone who has ever tried to enter a house through a brick wall will understand the importance of doors, windows or at least pickaxes.

Learn to spot the signs of blindness, embrace creativity, and stay active. If you can do that, you'll begin to recognize blindness in your perseverance and reduce wasted time.

BE CAREFUL HOW YOU MEASURE SUCCESS

My oldest son is an avid reader, but he needs help getting started with books. Often, his path into a book is through the film. We could sing with the chorus on this and harp on how screen time is damaging our child's brain, but Ashley and I believe reading is more important than not reading.

Without the Harry Potter movies, my son wouldn't have read the books. Because of the movies, he read them and passed the tests at school, and before you point to how of course he could pass the tests because he watched the movies, consider he was nine years old and read all seven books in four months.

It's funny to think how it all wouldn't have happened had I persevered in my initial stance. I originally said if he was old enough for the books, he was old enough to comprehend them without the films as a crutch.

I failed to understand how his brain worked, or what would engage him by proclaiming how it *should* work. Had I persisted in my misconceptions, trying for his own good to teach him to value reading over watching movies, I'd have withheld from him one of the great joys of his life.

My son's love for Harry Potter bloomed into a love for the Percy Jackson books, and as he had for Harry Potter, he needed to watch the movies first. But using what I'd learned about his thriving, I encouraged him to watch and was rewarded by his further love of reading.

Where are you displaying perseverance toward rigid ideals and holding yourself back from success?

Your head may be strong enough to break glass, but do you really want to test your skull that way? How many times do you have to crash into a barrier before you search for another way in? Wouldn't it be better to try varied approaches when we meet resistance?

Those who are innovating, reworking, and experimenting have the edge. You can't succeed without hard work, but without innovation, experimentation, and self-reflection hard work is a blunt tool at best. Beware the person who leans on hard work but lacks results. They use guilt and shame as motivators, and find pleasure in other's failures.

This can be a hard lesson to learn, but success is fast. If something is failing to produce results quickly, try something new. It's better to stop doing something decent to find something great than it is to stay the course and reap minimal rewards. Whenever someone tells you consistency is key or patient is a virtue, suspect them. The truly successful don't preach such nonsense.

It's not your fault if this perspective shocks you. Most of us were raised to believe perseverance was a display of character. Only, most of us haven't achieved greatness. What is it they say about the blind leading the blind?

If we can't adapt the way we think to embrace impatience and creativity as the fastest way to learn, we won't experience the kind of book sales we dream of.

USING SELF-REFLECTION TO SHAPE YOUR SUCCESS MINDSET

To develop a tenacious, succeed-fast, scale-big mindset toward your book sales, commit to asking and answering questions. Nothing moves you toward results faster than a tenacious curiosity. Here are some questions to get you started:

How many copies of your book do you want to sell before launch? In the first week? The first month? By the end of year one?

What feels like sacrifice to you? Do you view low book sales as a form of sacrifice? What are you willing to sacrifice to achieve your writing goals?

Do you view your book primarily as a work of art? How important is it to develop the entertainment level? Is it a tool for communication? Do you hope to use it as a tool for education or enlightenment?

Do you believe most anyone who gives your writing a chance will love it? Who is most likely to enjoy your book and why will it appeal to them? Who are the readers most likely to love your book? What will make a reader rave about your book and commit to sharing it with all her friends?

How do your views of the market for your book impact the way you plan to share it?

What are some unique ways you can share your book with future readers? How much money can you commit to the advertising of your book? Where do you have the most interactive audience? Where can you begin to create a deeper audience connection?

Where do you find the readers who will be entertained by your book, and how do you approach them so they understand immediately why your book is the best book for them today?

Do you view your book as an asset that enriches people's

lives both materially and emotionally? What is your definition of an asset?

The more you grapple with these questions, the deeper understanding you'll gain. Some inspiration will lead to dead ends. You might decide to try TikTok and find in a couple months that the platform drains your energy in profound and lasting ways. You might realize no matter how much you despise direct cold contact, it is the most effective method and can't be ignored.

The quicker you move through these questions, the faster you'll refine your personal recipe for success. The more often you review these questions the deeper you will understand your personal story and how it drives the sale of your book.

Quit efforts when they deplete energy or lack results. It's okay to move on, even if everyone tells you you're crazy for doing so. Remember, the goal is to learn fast, because velocity is your secret weapon when selling your books.

WHAT TWITTER TAUGHT ME ABOUT SPEED

Chances are decent you met me first on Twitter. But you might not know my story there is one of two speeds.

It is true I founded my personal account on March 14th of 2022, and it's true that by June 15th of 2022, my profile surpassed 10,000 followers. In ninety-two days, I packed on 10,000 followers, the vast majority of whom were readers and writers, or in other words, my target audience.

I detailed in two separate episodes of THE RELUCTANT BOOK MARKETER how I gained those followers, and since this book is a companion to the podcast, I'll let you find those episodes at your leisure and not repeat the story here.

However, one detail I've only hinted at before is the alternate profile that enabled me to move so quickly with my personal profile.

In 2018, I wanted to begin querying my novel, THE NINE LIVES OF MARVA DELONGHI, and I saw one gaping hole in my author presence: namely the total lack of an author presence. It was a bit like being the student who skips class all year and tries to cram for the final the night before the exam.

I'd never cultivated friendships in my city with other writers. I had a Facebook profile I never used and no other social media. Frankly, I hated social media, but I knew that had to change.

Given how unpalatable the idea of social media was, I pitched the idea of creating a profile as the main character of my novel. I've never revealed the handle before now: @LukeEMiaPI is me and my friend John G. We operated the profile together for a year and a half.

The growth was slow, and I rarely enjoyed the process. John ran it more frequently than I in the beginning, and I claimed from day one that I couldn't grow the following. I lamented how awful the experience was, but around the one-year mark, we crossed a thousand followers.

And I'm glad I had John to help me, because that profile helped me land my literary agent.

Then, during the winter of 2020, a year and a half into submission, my agent sending the book to editors, I began to realize my reach was too limited, so despite my distaste for all things social media, I got more serious about growing Luke's profile.

Shear dumb luck caused me to stumble on the power of questions. Each morning I'd schedule nine tweets, and I started noticing questions led to interaction and engaged followers more than anything else. I even had a handful of people tell me I asked great questions. If you don't respond to compliments, go get a cardiogram, because you might be dead.

Put all that in the brain pan, and in the winter of 2022,

after I started my podcast and ran into all kinds of resistance growing my listenership, I recognized a need to find people outside of my personal community.

You might expect I'd connect the dots, but I didn't. I tried to use Facebook groups to grow my listenership, but it was slow and the groups were filled with spammers, and I felt like a spammer, and it was bad enough using social media so much, but feeling spammy about it really stunk.

That's when my friend and fellow podcaster, Jeff came along. Remember Jeff? He told me he was using and having success with Twitter.

Cue the official lightbulb moment and symphonic overture!

I first wanted to use the Luke profile, which by that point had over two thousand followers, but I knew I couldn't promote the book and podcast without revealing who Luke was, and her audience and my audience were different people, anyway.

So I chose to start from scratch, which forced me to consider how I could grow a following. The first one hundred people I followed came from the profile of a group founder I'd interacted with on Facebook, and once I had a hundred followers, I relied solely on asking questions and answering people's responses.

The rest, as I said, you can hear about on my podcast episodes, but it's important to recognize that had I not spent several years failing at Twitter I'd not have stumbled on the power of asking questions there.

Asking questions paired with targeting specific people combined to make an amazing strategy. And when I hit on that strategy, I discovered targeted growth happens fast. It's the foundation of my success.

But how do you know when you've landed on a strategy that will fuel speed? You need to cultivate a mindset of self-reflection and integrity.

RUNNING SHOULD BE COMFORTABLE

Not long ago, I had a conversation with the founder of Xero Shoes. If you aren't familiar with zero drop shoes, or barefoot running, check the QR codes in the back of the book to learn more about Stephen Sashen's story and why these shoes can change your life.

The reason I'm mentioning Stephen here is because he spoke at length about what he called an affliction. He told me he's always gotten grief from the people in his life for running in all directions at once. Action creates mindset! Isn't it funny how successful people are doing things other people aren't?

Stephen summed up his method as building twenty bridges at once. He liked to create a map of all the possible strategies that could work to get in front of his ideal customers. When the map is done he starts building bridges to every possible outcome he's identified.

That approach has led Xero Shoes to be the most popular barefoot running brand, and the only shoe I wear. That approach is the approach that enabled me to grow a Twitter account at an average of 137 followers per day over the first three months of founding the account.

That approach is the approach that will give you a shot at selling a million books to a million fans and earn a seven-figure income. And if you're concerned that you don't possibly have the time or energy for a dozen bridges simultaneously, contemplate why.

START SMALL AND SCALE ACCORDING TO VICTORIES

If you think Stephen Sashen completes every bridge he starts building, you'd be tempted to think he had supernatural energy. The truth is, he has the same amount of energy as you. Maybe less depending on how carefully you maintain your diet.

Stephen doesn't finish every bridge. Some he accelerates as they prove promising. Some bridges he pours energy into, diverting his and others' time and resources there. Other bridges barely progress as he has time. Many he abandons.

Consider my approach to building a social media following. I began on Facebook, started with my own list of friends. I saw no measurable growth in my podcast audience after a few months and incorporated Twitter.

At the same time, I started TikTok and Instagram.

Using these social media channels, I tested various strategies to see what worked. Where did I get in front of the most writers and readers? When Twitter took off, I slowed interactions on Instagram and TikTok. For a time, I left everything else almost stagnant while I gave the lion's share of time to Twitter.

Simultaneously, I spent efforts on emailing podcast hosts to guest on their shows. When guest appearances had a smaller impact on podcast growth, I slowed my efforts to be a podcast guest, but I continue to pitch myself where it makes sense.

I also pitch guest blogs and newsletter announcement swaps. And these are things you will benefit from if you do them too.

Depending on your genre, your natural strengths, and your specific style of creativity, you may find success on Twitter, TikTok, LinkedIn, Instagram, Facebook, or elsewhere.

Moreover, you'll want to consider other strategies. Digital media is only part of marketing. How can you get in front of live people? Can you leverage relationships to book speaking opportunities or readings? How can you use the phone to connect with new readers, bookstores, and other retailers?

Where can you go to meet future readers? If you want to have seven-figure results, you need to find methods others are afraid to use both in familiar settings and in novel and unfamiliar settings. Remember, you can have a comfortable life, but you can't publish a bestseller without your best efforts.

CHAPTER
FOUR

VIEWING YOUR NOVEL AS ART DIMINISHES ITS VALUE

I WROTE the earliest short story featuring Bogey Morris in 2011. The book was meant to be a linked collection of shorts in the form of David Phillip Mullins' GREETINGS FROM BELOW[4]. Beginning as strictly flash fictions, each story was contained to one thousand or fewer words.

The limitation on what stories I could tell in that form led me to expand the story lengths. I spent my entire first year of graduate school writing these stories with the intent of using them as my thesis.

Then, during my review at the end of the first semester, second year, my advisor, Sam, told me my stories weren't working. He called the effort a complete failure—as in, start from scratch, buckaroo.

I raged. I wrote a scathing draft of an email telling Sam he simply didn't understand my artistic vision. I belittled his published books. Trash talk behind his back could've been measured in tons. I was petty in every imaginable way.

When the rage dried up, I reread Sam's comments and accepted his assessment. I asked myself, did I want to stand on my artistic soap box or did I want to write a book people loved. The answer came easy, because, as I've always said, what's the point of writing if no one is reading?

I scrapped the book, keeping only a few bits of the stories and rewrote the book as a braided novel of fictionalized memoir. If the last six words of the previous sentence made you scratch your head, you know where this is going.

I defended my thesis and graduated in the highest esteem. Sam told me I was going places. I managed to connect with his friend Joseph, author of TO ASSUME A PLEASING SHAPE[5], and get a direct recommendation to an agent who would read my manuscript when it was finished.

The agent spent all of ninety seconds with the manuscript and let me know it was too experimental and she didn't know where it would fit in the market. Devastation upon pain upon disillusionment heaped with resentment and hatred followed.

I drafted an email to send the agent explaining how she didn't have the first idea how much she'd regret passing me by when I sat atop the mountain built on the corpses of John Updike, Bernard Malamud, Alice Munro and William H. Shakespeare.

When the rage again subsided, I reread the agent's note, accepted her comments and placed the very artistic manuscript in a metaphorical desk drawer also known as a Dropbox file where it has lived untouched ever since.

I puzzled over what readers might want that I would likewise be interested in writing. And yes, we're going to get to a section drilling deeply into the mindset behind what readers want *that we are interested in writing*, but let's stay with artistic visions for now.

There will come a day for me, and for you if you remain determined and pliable both, when you can publish the solely-for-the-sake-of-art manuscript you've always dreamed of publishing if that's what you want when the day comes.

Until that day, you have a choice, and it's all about mindset. You can be true to yourself and write the artistic opus that few will read, or you can think about readers and write what they want that you'd be interested in writing.

A TRULY BAD EXAMPLE THAT'S TRULY TRUE NONETHELESS

You may have heard of Katy Perry. What about Miley Cyrus? These two pop musicians had roots in Christian music and used it as an avenue to mainstream success.

Perhaps they cling to their faith deep, deep, down in their faithful souls. Maybe not. Oh, and let's not forget Jessica Simpson. Christian labels have a lower barrier to entry than secular pop labels, but anyone who can sell tens of thousands of albums is going to get a decent look by any label.

These three musicians used the low barrier to entry as a way into the industry, and you might question their motives for doing so, but you'd be narrowminded to dismiss the outcomes. All three went on to record platinum albums and achieve mainstream success. You may not have a taste for their music, but you can't deny their talent.

Now, I'm not advocating for exploiting religion to climb the mountain toward fame, and I'm not suggesting any of these musicians are either, but I am using their path to success as an example of what is possible when you identify unique entry points to start your career.

Do you love thrillers? Are you a romance junky? Have you read every book by Michael Connelly and feel you understand the murkiest depths of mysteries and thrillers?

It so happens thrillers, romances, and mysteries are the top three selling genres in literature. Listen, if you love reading any of those genres, you'll love writing them, and if you love writing them, readers will love reading them.

Is there anything wrong with prioritizing publication? If not, write the best damn romance you can, follow it up with something slightly more character-driven, drop a third book that has a few uncharacteristic twists, and make a huge splash with your fourth book by leaving the genre for something you've always dreamed of writing.

Reinvention is a powerful career trajectory that gives artists more staying power than anyone talks about. Consider Radiohead. Or maybe you prefer to keep your examples in writing. Stephen King[6], master of horror, rarely writes horror anymore. Bernard Malamud[7] wrote a baseball novel followed by a dark comedy about a university professor.

Bill the Bard[8] wrote poetry, comedy, and tragedy. Patti Smith[9] is one of the most famous folk and rock musicians of the past sixty years, a renowned memoirist, a painter, an activist, and she's not just these things because she's famous. She's a crossover success, and you can be too, but you can't kick down doors with origami boots.

Roberto Bolaño[10] wrote poetry for decades before pumping out a dozen novels in the span of three years before dying of cancer. He wrote the novels so he could leave his children a legacy, and his novels are not only beautiful but sell prodigiously. He wrote to sell, and he sold like mad.

Andre Dubus Sr.[11] spent his career with little-known publisher Godine. When he needed money at the end of his life, he switched to one of the Big 7 (now the Big 5...soon to be the Big 4, it would appear), and got a huge payday.

Artists we all admire have woven in and out of the mainstream as needed, reinventing themselves along the way, and each of them, ultra-successful, understood the mindset that while some art appeals to fewer people, the passion projects serve as an anchor to create rabid, long-lasting fans. At bottom though, books are assets and need to be viewed as such.

ART IS AND ISN'T ALL YOU HOPED FOR

Art is for the uplifting of humanity. Art is emotional. Art is insightful. Art is expression. Art is unifying. Art is instructive.

For all of those benefits why do we feel so hesitant to ask others to buy our novels?

How much easier is it to recommend another's novel than it is our own?

Is your novel any less deserving?

The mindset we approach our own novel with has everything to do with how we market and sell it. If you believe your novel will bring entertainment, enjoyment, learning, and encouragement to a reader, you have a responsibility to share it with those who will benefit from it.

Once you see the value in your book, you will see it as an asset to give value to readers and to enrich their lives. If you deny readers that gift you are forced to confront that you are either a self-centered person or you don't value your book after all.

YOUR NOVEL IS AN ASSET

Some writers need to enter into the creative space with no thoughts of financial performance. If that's you, by all means, draft a novel with art and entertainment top of mind. Whatever your process is for getting the book drafted, don't change it if it's working.

During the creative process, let the book be what the book needs to be: a form of self-expression, a wild and unexpected story, an adventure, a discovery, the tale only you could write. But, after you've completed a draft and it's time to edit, rewrite and revise, it's time to put on your marketing hat.

Many with backgrounds in creative, higher education bristle at the idea of writing anything other than for themselves, but if you have a desire to sell your book, you have a responsibility to consider your reader. And if you can't write for a reader, stick to your moleskin journals and your dear diaries, but I'm guessing that's not really what you want.

Do your readers expect breakneck pacing? Will they want deep, complex characterizations? How tolerant are your readers toward descriptive passages? What level of steam do they expect, fluttering curtains or athletic and anatomical accuracy? Do you need to weave in thematic elements to your story or are your readers turned away at the first scent of propaganda?

These and many questions help you to reshape your creative, unique first draft into a book perfectly made for your ideal reader. It's no more a mystery if the ah-ha is revealed at the book's halfway point than it is a romance if the love interests end up apart on the last page.

Once the process of discovery is complete and you have your market identified, you begin shaping your book to delight those readers.

A SHMALTZY LOVE STORY

I first saw Ashley in 2008. We were attending the same church. She caught my eye, and I knew she was unattainable, too pretty, too stylish, too self-confident. I was not the kind of guy who succeeded in attracting women: shy, quiet, serious, and guarded.

Several years passed during which I dated another woman and the extent of my interactions with Ashley included a lunch with her and my friend Joe at Olive Garden. I remember the lunch because I sat next to Ashley in a booth and though she kept plenty of space between us, I could feel the warmth of her body next to mine.

Someday, I speculate scientists will discover when two people are romantically compatible they vibrate at similar frequencies, exciting electrons and spiking physical heat.

Anyway, I'm not a scientist.

In the winter of 2010, the woman I'd been dating asked for a break. At the same time, Ashley and the man she'd been dating broke up. She took a trip to Moab, texting pictures to our Bible study of her adventures.

This was before the advent of smart phones, so you couldn't see who all a person texted like you can now. I was under the impression those photos were specifically to me, and decided she was flirting, which I welcomed by offering an uncharacteristic surge of bravery.

I began replying, admiring the scenery, making attempts to be funny, generally acting a smitten fool. The day following Christmas, after weeks of texting, I asked Ashley if we could talk, and I expressed my interest. My exact words, she reminds me, were, "So…I really like you."

Let's skip past the part where she said, "I've never thought of you that way before. I need more time to consider it" and jump to the point where we got married.

Why tell this story? Partly because I'm proud to have somehow managed to attract a woman of Ashley's intellect and beauty. It certainly wasn't my wealth—I had thousands in credit card debt—or my good job—I had none—or my education—I'd started college late and was only halfway through my bachelor's when we recited our vows.

What I do know is that on our honeymoon I attempted to quit cigarettes. Over the first year, Ashley downsized her wardrobe by donating more than three fifty-gallon trash bags full of clothes. We did these things to appeal to each other.

During our eleven-year marriage, we've each changed toward each other a great deal, though some elements of who we are have remained, there has been a consistent leaning toward each other, working to be what the other needs, trying to appeal to the other.

WHAT MY SHMALTZY STORY HAS TO DO WITH YOUR MARKETING MINDSET

You may have a significant other, a spouse, or someone you've pined for. How much did you adjust to attract that person? While we're always told not to marry someone expecting *them* to change, we can't help but transform *ourselves* to enthrall them.

Think of your audience in this light. Your readers are the out-of-reach person you hope to attract, and if there's nothing wrong with spending hours learning what band your crush likes, what food she prefers, what stores she shops in and yes, what books she reads, why should you feel lowly for researching your ideal reader?

Moreover, if you work to appeal to your crush, and that is considered a good sign, why do we suddenly critique writers who write toward their ideal reader?

I spent twenty-five years of my life being me, interested in myself and what I wanted before Ashley came along. Who I was wasn't going to transform overnight. I smoked for another three years after we married, and I vaped still five after that. It was a long, challenging road to quit nicotine, and while it's one I'm glad to have conquered, it took work.

It felt like changing who I was to sacrifice that, and let me be clear, Ashley never asked me to quit smoking. She married a man who smoked and expected she'd always be married to a smoker, but at the same time, she was proud of me for quitting and glad I didn't smell like tobacco when I did.

This is your manuscript.

WHAT DAVID FOSTER WALLACE HAS TO DO WITH SHMALTZY LOVE STORIES & SACRIFICE

My favorite author is David Foster Wallace. He wrote INFI-NITE JEST[12], OBLIVION, CONSISDER THE LOBSTER and other books. He is known for a few things: voluminous vocabulary, philosophical writing, footnotes, a mix of high-brow and low-brow diction, and writing lengthy novels. The original INFINITE JEST is 1,079 pages.

For reasons I can't understand, I connected with his work instantly. He wrote an essay for the New Yorker titled "Ticket to the Fair". In it, he has a list of foods served at the fair, and the poetic, emotive, flowing harmony of that list won me over so fully, I all but tattooed my forehead with his signature.

I've read all of his books, many twice, some I've lost count how many times.

My thesis in graduate school was heavily influenced by his style, diction, philosophy, and structure. The thesis, you'll remember, that failed to attract a literary agent.

When I decided I wanted to publish traditionally, I chose to shelf my tribute to Wallace. It required me to leave behind the sweeping sentences, the five-dollar words, the footnotes.

I sacrificed part of what felt like me, but in pursuit of my ultimate goal, to publish, I've learned new ways to tell stories. The journey has given me new values, increased my knowledge and passion for literature.

I wrote toward readers. The choices I made were personal, and reflected my desires, but they also reflected my desire to be in conversation with readers. I cared about starting a conversation around something that entertained me but appealed to a marketable audience.

If you go open-eyed toward a book readers will love, you'll have to sacrifice parts of what you love, but it doesn't mean you aren't writing something to take pride in and to feel proud of. In fact, you may find, as you write toward your ideal reader, you'll create work you are more proud of than anything you've created before.

NOW THAT WE UNDERSTAND SHMALTZY LOVE STORIES LET'S RETURN TO ASSETS

Assets are defined as objects that have intrinsic value. With care and upkeep an asset increases in value over time. The most common assets are businesses, stocks/bonds, and real estate. Each of these asset classes steadily increase in value over time.

While assets can fluctuate in value over short durations, on sufficiently long timeframes, the value of assets increase.

Consider, there was a time when consumers could buy a book for a nickel, likely not in our lives! But now a hard cover of your favorite author is going to put you out thirty dollars after taxes.

There are used books on my shelves, in great condition, that are listed on the bar code as costing $14.99. If I were to sell one of those copies on Facebook Marketplace, I could command more than $500.00.

It's important to understand from a physical perspective how books, as a collectible object can increase in value when properly cared for if deemed sufficiently desirable.

But from an even more pragmatic perspective, when Amazon made popular the ebook some years ago, most ebooks sold for less than a dollar. Now, the ninety-nine cent ebook is a great deal and most authors will price their ebooks between $2.99 and $9.99, which the market supports.

Yes, your eyes may be glazing over, but stay alert. The movement of price is critical, the same product that used to cost a buck now has tripled in value just by the passage of time. That is the beauty of an asset.

Assets, at the very least, keep pace with inflation.

A HOUSE IS AN ASSET, & YOUR BOOK IS AN ASSET

Viewing your book as an asset reveals the long-term win in publishing, and helps cultivate the value of how you publish it.

I'll only introduce the concept here, but do you want to sign over the perpetual rights to your books in a contract with a publisher? If you choose to do this, ask yourself, who does the asset belong to?

As long as your novel is in print, you can generate sales that produce income for you, the author, and the price of your novel will increase in price as the value of the dollar wanes. Every time you publish a novel it is the same as someone building a new house. (And keep in mind, as a fiction author, you have this advantage that your book can be evergreen.)

You created an asset out of raw materials. If the book sold a mere 1,000 copies per year, you'd earn the equivalent of two month's rent but with no roof to save up for or broken toilet to fix. Do you see the power of that? Imagine a backlist of ten books all steadily selling.

WHY YOU *REALLY* WANT TO OWN A HOUSE

The analogy between books and houses is only beginning. In fact, it gets better. For example, ask yourself why everyone wants to own a house?

If you answered "So they can grow in wealth," you miss the deeper truth.

People want to own a house because homeownership is status, self-expression, and the perception of security.

People want to own your book for the same reason.

ANOTHER ANECDOTE ABOUT DAVID FOSTER WALLACE

Did I mention that *Infinite Jest* weighs about seven pounds? It continues to be among the most revered novels in the modern cannon. Those who read it are elevated into a certain status throughout the literary community, and those who can discuss it intelligently are respected.

That's because Wallace all but included the Oxford English Dictionary in his book as well as philosophical concepts proposed by men and women with unpronounceable names. The subjects, though by turns humorous and irreverent, are emotionally and mentally taxing. Most people who have bought a copy of *Infinite Jest* have not read it, but it sits proudly on their shelf.

You can likely think of other novels like that. Ulysses by James Joyce is one. Any religious text would count. Because owning a copy confers some of the same elements of status as having read it. It says to those who see it in its spot on the bookshelf, "Here is a serious reader who thinks profound thoughts."

That is what owning a house does. It says to those who know the person, "Here is a financially thriving person who is responsible and hard-working."

If you understand why people open their wallet, you understand book buying. Books are as much a status symbol as they are a companion. How can you leverage your reputation and platform to entice readers to value your book as a status symbol?

ASSETS PROVIDE PRESTIGE AND SO SHOULD YOUR BOOK

Think about where you live. You're either there because it's what you can afford, or it's the part of town you feel best reflects your values.

Perhaps you have children so you live where there is a big

backyard and a great school district. I live in a small, rundown home because I could purchase it cheaply. My family is in a small town of fewer than 1,500 people. I've chosen this because I value real estate. This town isn't the coolest place, but it's affordable, and my kids are safe anywhere they wander.

Maybe you're young and love the happening areas, like Benson around 64th and Maple in Omaha or Dundee around 49th and Underwood. Perhaps you enjoy urban and happening, in which case the Blackstone neighborhood is your jam.

These names and areas mean nothing to you, but if you think of Omaha as my target market, immediately locals understand where I'm referencing.

No matter where you are, people either want to live, eat, drink and be seen in those places, or they want to avoid those places, and the real estate costs accordingly.

Think of your book as a type of real estate. If it's poorly written, people might avoid it, but if it's well-written, it's somebody's ideal story. In the same way, my wife wouldn't be happy in Blackstone, your book won't appeal to everyone.

WHERE THE COOL KIDS GO - A STORY OF EARLY ADOPTERS

When I first moved to Omaha, the Blackstone neighborhood was a dangerous area to walk through at night. Most of the shops along Farnam Street were closed, many windows boarded. The corner bar at the end of the strip served as many knife wounds as it did Rueben sandwiches.

Over the course of a couple years, a few real estate investors started buying the rundown, brick apartment buildings for bargain prices. They renovated and updated, and rented the apartments, attracting artistic, young, curious professionals.

Soon, the shops were rented, and restaurants, bars, and

boutiques moved in. Within ten years, the area became the most coveted spot in the city.

This happened because the investors saw what Blackstone should be and they elevated it to match their vision. The earliest adopters were the same people who will be your first readers.

Early adopters gain esteem from discovery. They are the people you know who always try new restaurants. They wear clothes that seem out-of-step with trends, but that you soon see others wearing. They attend small venues to listen to start up bands.

The early adopters signal to their circle that something is up-and-coming. But they won't go where there is no value, no appeal, so you have to have the mindset to attract early adopters to your book.

THE EARLY ADOPTER MINDSET

It's discovery. It's curiosity. It's inquisitiveness. It's persistence. It's education.

Think about your friend group. Who's the one person that always seemed to know where the best new restaurant was. When you want to know a good new place to eat, who do you ask?

That's the person you need to find in your genre. But if you aren't well-read and consistently involved in the conversation, you need to get there. Spend time educating yourself in the writers of your genre.

Who's the leading voice? Who are the ones making a name for themselves at this moment? Who are the critics reviewing the emerging authors? Where are the podcasts discussing obscure works in your genre?

Because here's something you might miss if you aren't inquisitive: The critics discussing the writers' books you need to be reading might be mediocre critics. Same for the podcasts. You might find the podcasts interviewing the authors of interest are low-budget.

My podcast is low budget, which means most authors I speak to are early in their careers and haven't hit the mainstream. That's a sign, you're getting close to early adopters. My listeners are starting a journey, and if you share an audience, you need to attract the people who have gathered around me.

But you can't just pay to run an ad on my show. Instead, you have to show up where I'm spending time, engage with the people I engage with, bring value where you see I miss opportunities, and start to grow your community.

I won't hold it against you. There's plenty to go around, and I'm doing my best to bring value to everyone, so if I'm missing, it means I can't get to it.

Excite the people I overlook, and they will propel you to a larger audience.

WHAT IS IT THEY SAY ABOUT A FIRE HOSE?

Pop Quiz! Who are the most important people in neighborhood revitalization? If you answered early adopters, you're wrong. They're the audience, the target, the niche, the first subjects, but the **most important** people in neighborhood revitalization are the real estate investors.

If you want to be a bestselling, full-time novelist, you have to think the way real estate investor's think. That means learning to recognize value before early adopters. If that seems like a tall order, that's because it is a tall order. No one said the road to bestselling would be easy.

What I'm telling you is if you adopt the right mindset, this journey is reproducible. Anyone can do it.

By shifting your mindset you'll move away from what failing authors are doing and discover what successful authors do to sell thousands of books every week.

Through shifting your mindset you'll begin to expect hundreds, then thousands of books sold each month.

And once you've shifted your mindset, you're going to experience the freedom from seventy-hour workweeks that result in low to no income and free you to do what you do best: write the next novel.

DENIS JOHNSON THE COOL GUY

If you prefer clean language in your book, feel free to skip this illustrative story.

Denis Johnson wrote Jesus' Son. It is a collection of short stories and highly regarded by most in the literary community.

The main character of Jesus' Son is a man only ever referred to as Fuckhead.

Jesus' Son arrived quietly into the literary community, but over time it gained a cult-following—to which I proudly belong.

The book itself came out in 1992 and there are so few hard covers of it, that most people believe it never issued in hardback. Because of its scarcity, the most inexpensive first edition[13] starts at a $100.

As the book gained in popularity, there were those who read the book like poetry, keeping a copy on them for rereading at almost all times. And because of the book's compact size in paperback, it became common to see readers tucking the volume in the back pocket of their jeans.

You were a cool person if you had a pocket edition of JESUS' SON, and because the book became a status symbol, its value and cultural significance grew, giving Johnson one of the biggest names in literature.

RECOGNIZING VALUE

What mindset do real estate developers have that you lack? They recognize value. When novelists learn to recognize value, they prime their process for speed.

This is going to be hard to hear. It's perhaps the biggest mindset shift you have to perform, and I'm so willing to say it that if you throw the book or delete it from your device and give me a one-star review, I'm still going to say it:

You have to write with readers in mind.

WHY "WRITING FOR YOURSELF" IS AN INCOMPLETE MYTH

Before you rebut me and say that if you don't know anything else, you know one thing because Stephen King and Margaret Atwood and _____ said it: "You have to write for yourself," realize, I didn't tell you not to write for yourself. I didn't even tell you not to write what you know.

The absurd notion that the choice is either/or must be a cruel prank of the most hateful, jealous writer. We can write for ourselves and our readers. We can do both.

What none of the big-name NYT Bestselling authors manage to marry to their light and fluffy _write for yourself_ quip is that the heart of that truism has nothing to do with content. The very editors with the publishers who printed their books ensured the books were made for the reading public.

Let's consider the metaphor of exercise to help your mindset.

If you want to be a world class long jumper, how helpful will pushups be in bringing you closer to your goal? How about arm curls? Will the bench press get you there?

Hey, if you thought of exercise the same way you thought of writing novels, you'd be forced to say the lift didn't matter, just the fact that you were true to yourself.

EXERCISING FOR YOURSELF

Suppose you want to be a professional long jumper but you follow the same logic often preached in the writing community. Train for yourself. And because you don't enjoy squats or any kind of leg lifts, you decide to focus on pushups, arm curls, and pullups.

You train hard, for hours a day, but on the day of the event, when your turn to jump arrives, you place last, and tear your MCL in the process. Dejected, you ask how it could have ended this way when you worked so hard.

A fellow competitor mentions noticing you have a strong upper body but chicken legs and you reply that that is because you hate working out your legs. The competitor then says if you don't strengthen your legs, it's no wonder you can't jump far.

If you're a long jumper, you're going to have to jump every day. The hack sled is going to be your friend. Boxes will never be far away. Squat racks will be a way of life.

And on the day of the event, you're going to participate by the rules of the sport for the delight of the fans and your competitors. There's no other way about it.

Writing for yourself means doing it because you love writing. Writing for yourself means writing a genre you love reading. Writing for yourself means picking a schedule that works for you so you come to the desk as often as possible in the best mental, emotional, and spiritual shape.

Writing for yourself does not mean writing only when you feel like it. Writing for yourself does not mean calling your book whatever genre you want because that's how you think of it. Writing for yourself does not mean telling readers you like it and so they better like it too, or they're stupid and have bad taste.

You find the genre. You show up on schedule, and you commit to the story.

LITERARY FICTION IS NOT AN EXCUSE FOR MEDIOCRE SALES

Of all the genres, writers of literary fiction complain most about having the thinnest readership. And perhaps they do have a thinner base, but thin in this case still includes a massive 3,500 new readers per year and that's just counting MFA graduates.

Even adjusting for growth in attendance, by omitting the first decade of MFA enrollment 1940 to 1950, there are now 72 years-worth[1] of literary readers, meaning a conservative estimate of the audience for literary fiction would be around a quarter of a million readers in the United States.

Consider that any book which sells twenty-five thousand copies, just ten percent of the available US market would merit reprints, international distribution, and internal marketing and advertising, and the sales numbers on a first printing would explode. And now consider that the number of readers for the genre was limited to only college graduates and you can imagine the actual scale.

You simply need to find your niche audience, activate them, and create raving fans out of them…

CREATIVE LICENSE REQUIRES GENRE MASTERY

Suppose you write more mainstream genres, perhaps mystery. You need to read mystery: classics, modern, emerging. You'll benefit from reading criticism and reviews of mystery, by watching mystery film and TV. You want to go into any room and feel you know more about mystery than anyone there.

Learn the acts in a mystery. Learn the tropes. Understand your genre beat by beat.

It doesn't matter if you write an outline or fly by the seat of your pants, but it does matter that when you have a finished book you've created something that resembles the genre: shares the beats, shares the acts, shares the structure and the tropes.

Listen, when you know your genre front to back, if you want to bend, go for it. You'll delight and astonish readers if you get the blend correctly. My novel, *The Nine Lives of Marva DeLonghi* is a speculative noir. It's the speculative aspects that stopped my agent from tossing the book on the red X pile.

But if my agent hadn't been able to recognize the form of a hardboiled detective story immediately, all the playful elements of magic couldn't have saved it, because when the paint dries, this book is still a mystery and has to appeal to mystery editors.

THE CREATIVE COMMUNITY MINDSET

Even if you bend genre and think you've written something historically unique, you have influences. No one is a vacuum. This is another key mindset shift.

Your book may be a rare type, but it isn't one-of-a-kind. You have to let go of the notion your book is alone in the universe. Other books inspired you. Spend time reflecting on books, movies, TV, plays, commercials, social media and the natural world. Somewhere, you found inspiration.

By accepting your book as a stone in the river you position yourself to find the community that can help you launch your book to new heights. If you persist in demanding your work is unique, you will meet failure.

COMPS BUILD COMMUNITY AND COMMUNITY BUILDS BOOK SALES

If you haven't studied what I do on Twitter you should start. For being labeled the lowest converting social media outlet, I'm getting north of eight percent conversion on product promotion and I haven't spent a penny on boosting. I'm also pushing five percent engagement and running a million impressions a month. That's top-tier exposure and name recognition.

You'll notice the majority of my tweets are questions focused on book marketing mindset. But I also cultivate a handful of secondary communities. I'm slowly building an audience to market my novel to, mystery readers who appreciate the work of authors I drew inspiration from in my own writing.

Had I not been well-read in my genre, I'd struggle to know where my future readers were. And it's critical to have a clear notion of where our readers spend their time.

In my case, I began interacting with famous writers who currently have my audience and participate actively in the Twitter community. Gary Shteyngart is a key figure in literature my readers overlap with. Denis Lehane, Jason Starr and Daniel Kraus are others. Many of those who follow these authors stand a better than average chance of loving the work I'm writing, and so I spend time attracting those people into my community.

The difference between me, Gary, Dennis, Jason, and Daniel is that I respond to as many people as I can. I want to hear from my readers, my listeners, my friends and my fans. The other guys think it's enough to have a profile and to tweet the occasional thought. They respond only to the "worthy", those with credentials.

If you want to build the most productive, word-of-mouth, raving community, go above and beyond the Sheyngartian humor and engage with your followers. When they feel special, they feel loyal. And if you've ever watched THE SOPRANOS you know the power of loyalty. (Don't use your loyalty to kill people…unless I ask you to…I'm kidding…mostly…)

A WORD ABOUT CONNECTIONS

When you found, operate, and strategize for your own small business there comes a time when most of the people you interact with have connections to the business. It can be easy to slip off either side of the razor margin when your world is business.

On the one hand, you can feel guilty for viewing each person you speak to as a connection to someone else who can help grow your influence. On the other hand, you might be tempted to neglect established connections for new ones.

Running a business, writing books, marketing those books, advertising those books, all that comes with the territory takes so much effort it's easy to overlook the importance of the people who already love what you are doing.

If you want to have wild success, don't be afraid to collaborate with your connections to meet others who can help you along the way. There's no need for guilt. At the same time, be aware of the people you know and how you can serve them. Don't ignore people who are your readers for those who may be your future readers.

It's a simple mindset, but it's often the one writers most miss when growing a platform.

CHAPTER
FIVE

YOU ONLY DO the Things You Want to Do

Why do people know what to do, but refuse to do it? If you believe me, this has the ability to change the course of your life and define the way you spend the time you have left. It's the most important truth I can share with you, and in one way or another I've stated it many times already.

You only do the things you want to do.

WANT IS A TRICKY SUBJECT

You can tell yourself some people are born into worse conditions. Some people are born with less advantageous skin colors. Some people are born with genetic disadvantages. Some people are born in dangerous countries. Some people are born in the wrong body. Some people are born to love the wrong person. Some people are born the enemy of the ruling class.

But in all of the above conditions, people born into those trials have overcome by force of want.

I'm never going to say everyone faces the same obstacles. It helps to have a thin body and an attractive face. It helps to know how to speak persuasively. Some people are born with a natural gift to these things. It helps to be born into wealth, privilege, white skin, to be American, to be male. Without doing a single thing, I check many of those boxes just with my genetics.

But if you want something, truly want it, nothing will stop you, and if you don't want it, no advantage can persuade you to get it.

You may get where you want to go faster than your peers if you were born into the right situation: Paris Hilton, Colin Hanks, Miley Cyrus, Joe Hill. And if you can deny a single one of the people on this list displays massive talent, heart and energy, please make your case.

Success, being a household name, requires want.

If you want it, you can have it. But it requires you to want it more than you don't want it.

The first moment you say no, that is the moment you see how deeply your want runs.

EVERY TRUTH HAS A FAILURE

Self-forgiveness is important in this conversation. I've said no to writing before. I've said "I'm too sick, I'm going to bed early."

Other times, I've been dealt a rejection that bruised a unique pain spot and spun into a brief but gripping depression making writing seem futile and joyless.

I even spent a period of about eight months going through the motions without any effort to publish, connect with others, or move my writing forward in a meaningful way.

There are moments like these when you need to forgive yourself for losing course.

The road is long. The journey is littered with obstacles.

THE POWER OF DOUBT AND SURRENDER

In 2012, I held a middle management job for a general merchandise distributor. I traveled weekly in that role. One trip took me to Anchorage. I'd never been. Due to my inexperience, I didn't know how far in advance I needed to book a vehicle in Alaska and by the time I tried, there were no cars available.

I decided I could adlib. The route sales representative had a vehicle. He could pick me up at the airport, and I'd just have to ride with him for our few days of training.

The rep, though, was unreliable, which was the reason I'd booked travel to visit him. When my plane touched down, he hadn't returned any of my calls or texts.

I arranged an airport shuttle to my hotel and called my boss to say the rep was unresponsive.

My boss said, "You can't do anything. Keep trying to touch base, and in the meantime, have fun."

I really took the "have fun" part to heart. Some twenty hours later I was released from the drunk tank with a summons to attend court for a series of misadventures. Talk about unreliable.

So I walked out of lockup, and I found a concrete barricade, and I squatted in its shade, and I called my wife. We had been married for two years at the time.

She expressed all the fear and anger you would expect. Apparently, when you call your husband sixty times over the span of ten hours and the calls all land in the voicemail box worst-case-scenario thinking is reasonable.

I had a choice about how I would respond.

There was an option to deny that my behavior was a product of an ongoing and unmanageable addiction not only to alcohol but to theft and deception, or I could tell her I'd had a one-off bad stroke of luck.

I doubt your rock bottom looks like mine, but you can

think of a time when you hit a wall. Perhaps it was a brutal divorce. Maybe you spent so much on credit cards you had to file for bankruptcy. Possibly you hit someone in anger and were charged with assault and battery.

It could be a smaller offense. Maybe you were fired from a job. Somewhere, there is a moment when you were confronted with a horrible choice to admit your shortcomings and change course or let the truth hide and continue with the same behavior.

Whatever has come to mind for you in this moment, that memory will tell you how badly you want what you claim to want.

If you say you hope to sell thousands of books and earn a living as a novelist, but every time something arises that challenges you, you flee you're telling yourself what you really value.

You have a choice. If you don't want the sales, it's okay to walk away. Many have walked away and found a great deal of lightness in doing so.

Bitterness is worse than all diseases. It devours but never kills. Admit what you want, and aim your efforts at getting it, but if you say you want something, you have to do **whatever** it takes to get it. I can confidently say no action you'll be required to take to sell thousands of books will be as soul-pressingly painful as confessing not one, not two, but three MASSIVE character flaws to your spouse of two years.

As you might expect, I confessed what amounted to months of deception, throwing myself at Ashley's mercy. I'm so, so, so glad to say, we'll be celebrating our eleventh anniversary in seven days (as of this writing) and the past nine years have afforded me the opportunity to earn back her trust and make strides toward the publishing career of my dreams.

ANOTHER OPPORTUNITY TO WALK AWAY

I can say, I hope your story isn't so dramatic as mine. Many aren't. Some make mine look tame. The point is: you have a choice. Grab what you want and banish excuses. Embrace the mindset of a seven-figure author or define what success looks like to you.

Please, though, if you don't want to sell a million copies of your book, this book isn't for you. Put it down. Read something else. Everything I've written so far, you already know. This is simply a reminder for those, who like I did in 2019, momentarily lost the path.

You want this success? It's yours to have. You want this? Ignore that feeling like we're about to get woo-woo. This isn't woo-woo. Wherever you are, read this aloud: "I am willing to do what it takes to have the success I've always wanted."

A METAPHORICAL BLOOD PACT FOR SUCCESS THROUGH COLLABORATION

If you're still reading you've either failed to be honest with yourself about your writing goals, you are relatively sure you want to do whatever it takes to sell a million copies of your book, or you are all in, ready to do what it takes.

I'm talking to you. You're still reading, so I'm talking specifically to you: I commit to doing whatever it takes to give you everything you need to adopt the seven-figure author's mindset.

That is a job I committed to when I founded my podcast, THE RELUCTANT BOOK MARKETER, and it's one I want to do for the rest of my life.

Do you agree to face the uncomfortable bits I'm about to confront you with? Would you sign it in blood?

ACTION CREATES MINDSET

You can sit in your comfy chair or perhaps you're at work sneaking a read, and the chair isn't so comfy, but if you don't act, you can't reshape your mind.

You're likely going to hate this exercise, and for most people, this is the worst possible thing they can think of. If you're anything like I have been at times in my life, you'll read through this exercise to the next part, vaguely committing to return to it after you've gotten through the whole book.

(Don't do that!)

You're going to ask, "Can't we work up to this?" and I'm going to reply, "No. Because if you can't do this, it's not worth wasting your time with easier tasks because you have to be able to do this to have the seven-figure marketing mindset.

Let's hope the suspense is killing you.

Your first exercise is to take five copies of your book (if you've published) and carry them with you as you knock on ten strangers' doors. If you have no published book you need to carry a QR code that links to your mailing list.

If you don't have a mailing list, you need to create one now and if you don't know how to create QR codes, search online. And lastly, if you don't live in a neighborhood that feels safe, please go where you can feel safe knocking.

Knock on ten doors and ask these people to buy your book or sign up for your mailing list.

A WORD ON TARGET AUDIENCES

Let's do away with the excuses. We all know the ten houses you visited with your book or mailing list were likely not your target audience. It doesn't matter, because it forced you to confront the natural revulsion you've built up around being that "nasty salesperson" everyone hates.

We'll address the mindset behind that viewpoint you've unconsciously reinforced your whole life, but not before we overcome the hesitance to act. Action in the only way to propel yourself forward to the kind of reach you strive for.

If you couldn't knock on ten doors, you must renounce the claim that you want to sell a million copies of your book. And if you're fuming right now and making every excuse as to why your graduate school thesis is a brilliant work of art you...

Wait...

What's that?

Wrong story. Yes, my mistake. If you're feeling upset, angry even, it means I've struck a note, and you do want to succeed, but the price is shocking. Here's your second chance. Ten neighbors await. Don't walk away until they open the door.

(And for the reader who's still reading but has consciously chosen not to knock on doors because it's a waste of time or because you're convinced you know better, I have a question for you: how does it feel to live being hopelessly self-deceived and hopeless. Thanks, I guess, for at least buying my book.)

OBSESSION FOLLOWS MONEY

Are you ready for another exercise in marketing mindset? It's time to put your money where your mouth is, and by money, I mean real money.

If you have a published book, go spend $100.00 or that equivalent in your local currency on advertising. A great ad to buy is Amazon. You can get quite a few impressions bidding on ads with a hundred dollars.

Feel free to research the best keywords and methods to make the ad most successful, but don't spend days on learning targeting. Action is your friend. Refinement comes later.

By the way, I know a few of you out there are shaking your heads. Who do I think I am asking you to spend $100.00 when you can't spare $5.00?

Throw the book out. Find someone else to listen to, because I'm telling you, you can't say you don't have the money. If you don't have the money, find a way to earn it. Put in a few hours overtime at work. Borrow it. Put it on a credit card.

I'm not encouraging financial irresponsibility, and I'd almost always advise you avoid credit card debt, but when action creates mindset, and money is many people's sticking point, we need a course of radical action.

If you can't do whatever it takes to find that money and spend it on your book, you must renounce the claim that you want to sell a million copies of your book.

And, listen, I'm fully aware there are dozens of free marketing options you can do to generate book sales, but no one sells a million copies of their novel with no ad spend. You have to accept the cost of doing business or it's pointless to keep moving forward.

If you feel I'm trying to push you away, you are correct. When you read this sentence, you're committing to staying engaged, and that commitment is building your mindset too.

Unpublished Authors, Not So Fast!

Those of you without a published book, you thought you got away without opening your wallets. Sorry! Not the case.

You need to go out and spend $100 on something that will improve your marketing knowledge. Buy marketing books like this one. Find a marketing course or a ticket to a marketing event. Get out and buy a marketing professional some dinner. Learn from those who've been where you want to go.

If you don't know where to start, let me recommend a few great investments: Grant Cardone wrote BE OBSESSED OR BE AVERAGE[14]. You'll recognize plenty of his mindset in this book. THIS IS MARKETING by Seth Godin[15] is a great marketing action book. Or get an in-depth class with Becky Robinson, host of The Book Marketing Action Podcast[16].

Nothing you spend money on will be a waste because the principle is to move your mind by pushing your money. We are emotionally wired to care about the things we financially invest in.

CHAPTER
SIX

JOURNEYS ARE MALLEABLE, SUCCESS IS PLANNED

NOW THAT YOU'VE got money in the game, and an idea of how unconventional entrepreneurs view their work, let's focus on why action creates mindset.

The goal in spending money on your book or marketing knowledge is to reshape not only what you think but how you think about it. Somewhere along the way, likely because traditional publishing has always been "free" to authors who sell their book, authors got the idea that publishing their book should be free.

That has led to poor thought processes and misleading assumptions. You need to reshape your mindset by training yourself to associate elements of marketing with financial investment. Money brings fear, clarity, urgency, and honesty.

Once you realize spending on your marketing education, on book publishing, and on advertising bring returns, you begin to open your wallet on instinct. And what's that feeling you're feeling when you swipe the credit card? Is it a sense of giddy satisfaction?

If you doubt me, answer this question: If I asked you for a dollar today, and in return, I'd give you two dollars tomorrow, would you give me a dollar? Would you view it as a loss, a loan, or an investment?

If you refuse that offer, you're beyond help. Even if a dollar was all you had to your name, you'd be illogical to refuse the deal, because just about anyone can go a day without. And after the initial investment, you'd have seed money to repeat the deal day after day for the rest of your life.

If I asked you for $5,000 today in exchange for $10,000 in two months, would you take it? If you say no now, you are only harming your future. If you believe in your own book you can ever spend the money on a credit card, right? You don't have to spend any of your own.

RETHINKING TRADITIONAL PUBLISHERS

The low-down, dirty, no good traditional publishers have defrauded authors for hundreds of years! In the name of convenience and expertise, authors have ceded the rights to their books, many times in perpetuity.

And if you've bought into the ideas in this book, you're beginning to see your novel as an asset, a property with the ability to earn you money for the rest of your life, but if you sign the rights away, it's no longer an asset. Would that be worth it to you?

I am not only willing to, but targeting the sale of my novel to a traditional publisher. I don't actually believe trad-publishers are defrauding authors. What I do believe is that many authors misunderstand the process at an almost criminal level and like any good business, publishers take advantage of author ignorance.

Because of that, the traditional publishing model has cultivated a hyperconcentrated gap between the top 1% and the bottom 99%. Perhaps this is a familiar success gap. If you want to be in the top one percent, you need to think like the one percent think.

Unless you're the author of a "most-anticipated novel of the year" you'll not receive a robust marketing push from your publisher. You'll have to fight to land on bestselling lists. You'll have to book your own tours. All of this marketing thrust will cost you money and time to tour the country reading your book to strangers while working on the next novel.

Meanwhile, one-percenters will have their marketing done for them, and because they do, they'll earn large sums of money and access to well-connected people. You'll have to push every ounce of the way expecting only the results equal to your efforts, and if you focus on the action, maintaining the mindset, you can turn the course of your journey beyond bestselling.

When you start as a first-time author with a meager advance of $5,000, you'll be tempted to sock away the money, assuming it's your earnings for the past several years of work.

But if you want to overcome the setbacks of being an unknown with an unknown future, you have to see the advance as funding for your marketing budget, a loan on copies to be sold. Treat it like that, and you can build a successful marketing plan to outsell your advance, ensuring a second book deal, and even earning a future income.

If it's any consolation, by simply outselling your $5,000 advance, you'll already have risen to greater success than 95% of other novelists. You might be tempted to think that speaks poorly of the publishing industry, and I'd have to agree, but it's certainly a start.

NOT SO HUMBLE BEGINNINGS

Let's face it. You aren't reading this book because your forth-coming novel is the most anticipated book of the year.

Chances are, if you are published, you signed a contract with a small press or you have chosen to self-publish. Both are exceptional paths and position you to reach a vast audience, earning large sums of money. And if you embrace the seven-figure marketing mindset, you can even push your success so far you cause your publisher real supply and demand issues.

The actions you'll take for small press and self-publishing will vary regarding specifics, but the mindset is the same. The mindset for success never varies. Accepting that leads to success wherever you go.

ACTION CREATES _____

Are you ready to act for your future of your marketing mind-set? Find a mirror. Look at yourself. Say to your reflection, "I am not a household name."

Stay with that statement until it bothers you. If you have to repeat the phrase, do so.

When it bothers you, say to your reflection, "It is in my control to be a household name."

Stay with this moment until you believe both statements. It is likely you will feel awkward doing this, and some of you may have memories of Stuart Smalley while speaking to your reflection. It's okay. Do it anyway.

Some actions people take are viewed as absurd but are useful. This is one such behavior that is useful. You will find it hard to lie to yourself when looking in the mirror. And you will find it hard to live with yourself when you aren't the person you expect yourself to be.

KEEP THE ACTION GOING BECAUSE ACTION CREATES MINDSET

Let's take another mindset shifting action! You've been the Founder, CEO, Assistant, Janitor, Public Relations Department, and Human Resources for your author house.

If something needs doing, you've been the one to do it. Harry Truman would theoretically be proud of you because for all your writing life, the buck stopped with you.

But today, we're going to change that because culture taught us to admire Harry Truman's view of responsibility too much. Being the sole task manager of your business—yes, writing is a business—has to stop today. You can sell a million copies of your book, but it won't be a solo journey.

Your action is to find an assistant and hire him to take one task off your plate. Places like Fiverr or Upwork can be a good start.

If you have a published book, you might hire the assistant to pitch you as a guest on applicable podcasts. The assistant might respond to all emails to your professional email account and provide a daily summary of action items that require your personal attention.

The range of tasks you can hire an assistant for are endless. You can find them inexpensively, but the most important element is to train your mind to value time more highly. Most of us have unconsciously taught ourselves to undervalue our time, which leads us to reinforce self-limiting beliefs.

Look at where you are spending time on mundane or easily repeatable tasks and hire the most repetitive work out to an assistant. If you're worried about the cost, push yourself to find a task you can do to earn that money. If you can earn more money than the cost of hiring the assistant, you'll doubly reinforce the power of diversification.

And if at first, you don't see the return in value, spend

time learning how to get better results working with an assistant rather than assuming the process is flawed.

SOME WORK IS MORE VALUABLE THAN OTHER WORK

The old saying, "Eighty percent of results come from twenty percent of actions" might be as fluid a statistic as any in the collective public, but there's truth in the mindset even if the numbers are estimations.

If you can't see the path to earning a million dollars, reaching a million people, and selling a million copies, you haven't embraced this mindset.

And why are you wasting your time reading this book if you're already on the path to a million dollars on your published books? Thanks, I guess, if you decided to see what all the smoke was about…

You likely understand where you're wasting some of your time, but the radical mindset shift we need to work on is escaping the "slightly effective" for the "radically effective".

HIRE YOUR WAY TO FAME

Gig work is great and all, but can you imagine hiring a full-time employee to help you sell your book? What would happen if you put an executive assistant on staff to improve your efficiency, schedule your meetings, book your readings and appearances, declutter your life and drive your time so you wasted none?

Thinking small will have you scared at the prospect. You'll rip off all the standard excuses. How can I afford to pay someone else when I can't afford to pay myself? If I can't sell a book now how should I expect I can train someone else to do it? Blah, blah, blah.

If you want to level up and drive sales, you take the

plunge and worry about the logistics later. It sounds counter-intuitive, but all the best in business risk the most with the greatest self-confidence. When your choices are solve or fail, you'll be surprised how creative you can get.

But this is long enough in rarified air. Only one, perhaps two, of all my readers will take this advice. The good news is. The one who does will have a seven-figure book within twelve months. The commitment is that powerful.

THE CAR MECHANIC'S DAUGHTER

My car mechanic friend has a daughter who struggled with health problems as a child. Her digestion caused her no end of discomfort and embarrassment. She felt tired and struggled focusing at school. She constantly fought a runny nose.

My friend decided to take his daughter to the doctor after an unexpected restroom accident at school one fall.

The doctor ran a few tests but found nothing obvious. Based on his conversation with my friend, they decided to send the daughter to an allergist.

The allergist ran a series of pinpricks on the little girl's forearm, the usual suspects: pollen, dairy, nuts, seeds, and a handful of grains. None returned problematic results so the allergist worked with my friend's family to build a detailed menu of the foods common to their household.

They created a full menu of all the ingredients used in their cooking and emailed it to the allergist's office. Then, over the course of a month, the allergist's office sent instructions to rotate the ingredients out of use until the daughter showed improvement.

I remember my friend telling me how wildly tedious and frustrating the process was. He said it was hard at times not to just live with whatever the issue was. There was plenty of fighting and confusion all around.

Then, somewhere in the fifth week, my friend's daughter had a breakthrough. She awoke clearheaded, energetic, well-slept, and with a calm stomach. She could breathe easy. It happened all at once.

My friend called the allergist's office and shared the good news. They'd narrowed his daughter's allergy to one of five ingredients.

A couple days later, my friend discovered his daughter was allergic to oregano. It shouldn't have been a surprise, given the family's fanaticism about oregano. They added it to just about every recipe, but it never occurred to anyone that such an innocuous herb would have such a profound impact.

Strange as it may seem, the family struggled to let go of the beloved herb. Spaghetti sauces tasted flat, breads bland, lasagna too tart. Even the daughter missed oregano, but she didn't miss the stuffy nose and the classroom threat of bathroom accidents.

THE DILEMMA THE MECHANIC'S DAUGHTER POSES TO EACH OF US

Chances are, if you aren't finding the success you dream of, you have something making you sick, something you consume on a regular basis that dulls your senses, overwhelms your instincts, and hampers your efforts.

You might have to hunt for it, or you might know what it is. My mother's wife was lactose intolerant and yet she often chose to eat cheese and ice cream. She loved the flavor so much the digestive pain and brain fog were acceptable casualties for her until she took it too far and found herself laid up in bed.

Yet no matter how often the cycle repeated, she eventually returned to the dairy train. Perhaps you relate. You might feel like the mechanic's family felt, that your life is drab without the very thing that's holding you back.

Perhaps it's Netflix. Maybe it's scrolling Instagram reels or consuming news rather than creating it. It may be something else and you might not know what it is, but if you find it, and remove it, personal transformation is not far off.

SUBJECTIVE IS AN ILLUSION

I used to submit my short stories to literary journals on a regular basis. Most times I knew the journal had rejected me after three months of silence. Other times I'd receive a form rejection with a fluffy, *No Thanks, this one isn't for us, but we know this process is subjective.*

The only people who believe in subjectivity are the people who haven't dominated their genre, their market, and their life. Somehow, we're deceived into believing art is some mystical alternative universe that defies the laws governing the rest of reality.

If the Buffalo Bills score more points than the Miami Dolphins, is the winner subjective? If you eat cake every day and cause yourself Type 2 Diabetes, is your disease subjective? If you are pulled over for driving 90mph in a 75mph zone, is you speed subjective?

You only think art is subjective because you haven't identified the item or items that keep your art mediocre. Perhaps you possess stellar skills of prose but lack mastery of plot. Maybe you understand story but are lazy about grammar. It might be that you are a stellar storyteller with great style and grammar, but you have done nothing to be a great marketer.

Somewhere inside the process, you objectively lack the necessary skill to be objectively great. The sooner you accept that, the sooner you can fix the problem and see your writing dreams come true.

Instant Success Happens by Design

I used to carpet bomb every literary journal I could find

with submissions of my short stories. One story might go out thirty times before I trashed it or it got accepted in a journal. Often it was many months between submission and acceptance.

Then, on occasion, a journal would snap up a story the day I submitted it.

I spent years believing the stories that went in a day were strokes of good timing. Pure luck. I never compared what made those stories and submissions different or better than the others because I believed the subjectivity nonsense.

Now I know the difference. And let me be clear. Many, many literary magazines and journals are equally vague in their guidelines and stated preferences. You're no the only one who thinks the process is subjective.

But, do you know what made those stories get accepted so fast? It's easier than you think. Those stories were good. They were well-written, unique fictions, and they were perfectly targeted. Not that I had a clue about the targeting. That part was luck by volume, a lot like selling your book door-to-door. Hit enough doors and you're going to hit the target a few times.

I think we'd all agree, there are more efficient ways to do things. (Though if given a choice between efficient and active, you should choose the latter everytime.)

The problem is, you don't know you're targeting perfectly unless you're reading the journals you're submitting to, and it's a safe bet you aren't reading those journals, because the number of readers those journals have is in the low three-figures or high two-figures on average. And yes, you read that right: The average literary journal sells between 75 and 150 copies per issue[1].

If you want to increase your literary journal acceptances, improve the ratio of yeses to nos, and validate your ego, start reading the journals and target the right ones for you.

But also, ask yourself if it makes sense to spend your time gaining publications in the pages of journals next to nobody is reading. I think I can come up with about a bajillion better uses of my time, though I sympathize with any of you who just adore the sense of prestige gained from an elitist byline.

Targeting. The point is targeting. If you never spend time reflecting on that part of the process, you may never connect the how with the why.

Anyone can throw a dart at a dart board and hit the occasional bullseye, but only those who train rigorously can do it at will. If you want the kind of success uncommon to novelists, you have to learn to target both obstacles and advantages.

When I pursued lit mag credits, I wasted so much time with my spray and pray method it stuns me to recall. I could've written novels—plural—in the time I wasted on untargeted submissions. At least I could've read the publications I was seeking membership in to better know the type of stories they published.

When I stumbled into stupid blind luck, SBL as my grandpa used to call it, what a difference it made! Doors flew open when I sent a story to a journal that published work like the stuff I wrote. But I didn't learn. I persisted in believing as long as my stories had clean prose, compelling characters, and gripping stories, anybody would be awed—the rest would take care of itself.

You know what was even worse? I ignored readers. When I got readers, which was rare enough in itself, I ignored their feedback. If they didn't gush about my writing, I blamed them for having poor taste. If you're thinking I sounded delusional, you're thinking right!

So much of my work in those days was rushed, underdeveloped, and overwritten, but I was feeling too desperate to bulk up my CV to honestly evaluate my work's readiness.

Only because inspiration visits us all equally did I ever publish anything, because I certainly hadn't spent the time needed to learn how to elevate my writing for an audience.

I justified that planning, data-driven research, and selectivity didn't come naturally to me, so I chose to do what did come naturally. Knowing what I know now, I could've published ten times as many stories with a tenth of the submissions if I'd focused on writing for my audience and building relationships.

MAKE FRIENDS NOT FANS

When you're the best writer in your genre, you won't be able to avoid having fans. Your email inbox will be stuffed with notes of praise, adoration and love.

In the meantime, make it your mission to have zero fans. Instead make friends. It will start slow, but you're going to hear from people whose lives you've touched through your work. You could let those moments escape without building a friendship, but the seven-figure mindset understands the value of engaging with every person and taking interest in him.

See, a fan will recommend your book when given the chance, but a friend will go out of his way to tell people what you do, and that expanded reach has no boundaries. The same philosophy can fuel your book marketing plan with Star Trekian warp core fusion.

If you've ever submitted to a agents or editors, you're familiar with the slush pile. It's where unknown writers go to die. Sure, you'll get a rare acceptance out of the slush, but lightning is more likely to strike than you are to get a yes from the slush.

Yet I'm guessing you never worked to befriend an editor before. We're trained to leave editors alone, told it's intrusive to make contact and that may be true when you're on submission, but nothing is stopping you from connecting the rest of the time.

Imagine your phone rings, and you answer the call, and the person on the other side says, "Hey, I know we don't know each other, but I really need help packing and moving from my apartment to another place." There's a minuscule, insignificant chance you will say, "Oh sure I'll help you move."

But slightly change the situation and you're almost guaranteed to help that person move. Instead of a stranger calling, the person is your best friend or the woman you hope to marry one day or the man of your dreams.

If you are willing to help a dear friend move and at great expense to your leisure and time how much more do you think an editor who considers you a trusted friend is willing to publish your story in her literary journal?

But nepotism! Nepotism! you might be thinking.

All I can say to that is it sucks when it's not you. As you grow your influence, there will come a time when the one-on-one will no longer be feasible. That's when targeting goes from useful to critical.

SUCCESSFUL AUTHORPRENEURS TARGET FIRST

Listen to successful author entrepreneurs like Gary Vaynerchuk, Russell Brunson, Pat Flynn, Liela Hormozi or Grant Cardone and you'll hear a theme: If forced to start over, in a short time, they'd recoup everything they lost in short order. That's because when you know how the system functions, you recognize the patterns of success and implement them quickly.

In other words, they learn to target.

Gary Vee didn't stumble into a secret algorithm hack—he

devoted massive amounts of time to helping people, posting thousands of hours of video on YouTube and elsewhere. He went anywhere new social media platforms popped up.

Russell Brunson didn't invent Funnel Hacks as a reaction to accidental success. He studied how relationships were built, noticed the patterns and repeated those processes until he'd perfected them. Another way to say that is he targeted processes.

Pat Flynn didn't start Smart Passive Income by flipping a coin. Rather, he took a shocking moment of unexpected vulnerability and turned it into an opportunity never to be caught unprepared again. Another way to put that is to say he targeted fear and turned it into knowledge.

Leila Hormozi didn't settle for the meek and mild wife trope. She said no to stereotypes and devoted herself to uncommon ambition and goals. She went from having nothing to being on track to be the youngest female billionaire of all time. In other words, she targeted uncommon success and settled for nothing less.

Grant Cardone famously says he writes bestsellers not "bestwrittens". He holds it as a badge of honor that his first book had typos and grammatical errors and still made the New York Times Bestseller list. His aim is to publish books with clear thinking about how to achieve our goals and put them in the hands of his readers. In other words, he targets relationships with success-minded people and ignores critics.

If that all sounds exhausting to you, that's because the work these businesspeople are doing *is* exhausting: not every moment, not every day, but it does require gargantuan amounts of effort. Seven-figure mindsets demand massive action. You either choose to embrace the challenge or accept the limitations of balance.

I could scale back my interactions on Twitter. I could scale back from two podcasts episodes a week to one. Doing so would undoubtedly give me more balance, but no one promised balance came with the seven-figure mindset. In fact, the seven-figure mindset is a commitment to absurd, sustained imbalance.

IT'S HARD WORK BUT MORE GRIT

Hard work is great. You'd be challenged to find people who don't admire their ancestors for the sunup to sundown labor it took to run a farm, or pull coal from a mine. We still honor hard work today in all the men and women who struggle through military basic training. It's something highly idealized in many cultures.

But when we think of hard work we also think of single moms pulling two jobs, sleeping never and raising children. We think of underpaid overworked teachers. We think of retail jobs and cubicles, and somewhere in there we begin to equate hard work with soul-weary.

The mindset you need to sell a million copies of you novel and to transform a million lives looks nothing like soul-weary. What makes it different?

It's grit. Grit is defined as firmness of character and indomitable spirit. Can someone have those qualities if they don't see the purpose of it all? If you're just trading time for money behind some cash register, you'll feel weary, but if you understand how today's trials lead to owning the store and employing the person operating the register, that spirit becomes a lot firmer.

Grit it the key that transforms hard work into such an enjoyable process you forget it's hard and come to crave the striving. It's the vision than binds today's effort with tomorrow's rewards.

You will have to work hard, but far less often than you'll have to challenge your internal governor. Our brains are evolved to pursue safety and comfort. Hard work tends to reward us with both, but hard work rarely benefits us with excess, because excess demands uncomfortable work, and if our bodies hate one thing more than all the rest, it's discomfort.

When you force yourself to practice uncomfortable tasks, you'll find it critical to have your vision close at hand. Even still, understand, daily discomfort exhausts people far faster than anything else. It is the most challenging environment, which is why so few people succeed to the levels they once dreamed.

PUT ALL YOUR EGGS IN ONE BASKET

One of the most important times in my life followed being fired from my job managing the coffee shop at Immanuel Hospital. Healing Grounds it was called. Clever name, right? And ironic that getting booted from Healing Grounds is what began a kind of healing in me.

As an aside, I've been fired more times than many people have been hired. I was an opinionated, egotistical, take-no-orders kind of employee who struggled with managers and taking direction. To learn, I've needed excessive humiliation. I never played well with others. Add to that my appetite for excess, and all too often my judgement has been clouded.

I've no-showed on jobs because I could not mentally imagine the agony of enduring a six-hour shift. I lost an upper-middle-management position for choosing to fight with my boss. My foibles in the world of work are infamous and much gossiped about.

And so, following my being fired from Healing Grounds, I began a season of soul-searching. I concluded I needed to work at a wilderness therapy program for troubled youth. As a teen I'd been troubled, and I wanted to give back.

I'm sure the logic is sound. We'll just leave it at that…

The first of a series of life-changing lessons came to me

through that process and they will help you cultivate your seven-figure mindset.

The company I wanted to work for was called Second Nature. They had three locations. One in the Blue Ridge Mountains of Georgia, one in the Uintah Mountains of Utah and the other in the Cascade Mountains of Oregon.

I set my sites on getting a job at the Cascade Mountain location near Bend, Oregon. The Pacific Northwest had long appealed to me, and I had fond memories of nearby Portland. With that in mind, rather than looking for other similar programs to apply for, I chose to put, as my grandma would say, all my eggs in one basket.

Did I mention how, as a young man, I was notoriously stubborn—only in a dozen other places throughout the book, right—but the choice to wait on Second Nature only was bull-headed even for me. I cannot recount for you how many long conversations I had with my grandmother as she urged me to have backup plans in case my first choice didn't work out.

I refused to hear it. And, eventually, the call came.

Second Nature wanted me to drive out for an interview so I loaded up my credit card with purchases of outdoor gear, bought a car that could handle the miles, and set out for my adventure.

Though my grandmother has always been the centrally most important parental figure in my life, to this day I maintain she has missed out on a life of greater riches through an overactive abundance of caution.

As a writer, you're going to face similar dilemmas when you must choose to defy conventional wisdom. Perhaps you'll be determined to publish traditionally despite the advantages of debuting as a self-published author.

Maybe you'll have to stand firm on an editing decision for one of your novels that all your peer readers think should be changed, but I guarantee a moment will come where you will have to look at the world and say, yes I am putting all my eggs in one basket because it's the only sane choice to make.

KEEP AN EYE OPEN FOR OTHER BASKETS

On the face of it, this sounds like a contradiction. What's the difference between spreading out your eggs and having multiple baskets? To reapply a lesson from Mark Twain, the difference between the two is the difference between lightning and the lightning bug.

I arrived in Bend with certainty I would get the job at Second Nature and go on to enjoy years of satisfying work helping youth recover from bad decisions and enjoy brighter futures. Instead I immediately clashed with the trainer who was interviewing me and a handful of other candidates for the camp counselor position. He never told me as much, but I am convinced he too had had a troubled youth, and I think we vibrated on too similar a frequency.

Immediately, he sniffed out my hot-tempered side and he pounded on that button until it broke and started throwing sparks. I will never forget role-playing with him in the role of the troubled student and me as the counselor that day.

We had been instructed during those role-plays that if we became confused or needed guidance on how to handle a situation we could raise our hand and say, "Pause."

During a particularly tough situation I chose to do that. The counselor instructed me on how he might approach the situation, and we reentered the role-play.

He, in the role of the student, proceeded to contradict what he said the student would do. Then he, in the role of the student, began making disparaging comments about my physical appearance. I knew what was happening, but I couldn't stop myself from feeling betrayed and infuriated.

It wasn't being called ugly or having my rosacea criticized that angered me. It was that I'd trusted the information the trainer gave me, and he used that against me. I popped off and started raising my voice, failing to resolve the role-play.

The counselor called an end to the training for the day, and it was obvious I missed the cut. We spent one more night camping in the wilderness before returning to the office in Bend.

The counselor let me know he'd not be recommending me for a position in Bend, but he said there was an opening, and they would hire me if I was willing to relocate to Duchesne in Utah. I wanted to be near Portland. It had been a dream of mine since my early teens.

I asked if I could have time to consider. They said I wouldn't be needed in Utah for two weeks either way. I thought about my basket and my eggs. The situation made no sense to me.

I knew I had gone where I was supposed to go but the outcome was not the one that was supposed to happen. Driving across the divide to the lush green west coast of Oregon, I tried to comprehend all that had happened.

For a couple days, I searched for work in Portland. A man offered me a job throwing newspapers, but it wouldn't pay enough to earn a living. I'd worked in restaurants before, but that wasn't a world I was eager to revisit.

So I called Second Nature in Utah and told them if they were still interested I'd like to take a job there. To this day, I still view this time in Utah as some of the best of my life. I learned, grew, and matured in ways I never could've imagined.

Had I been stubborn about the location, like I was about getting the job at Second Nature, I would've missed some of the most enriching experiences of my life.

Being all-in doesn't mean charging blindly. Maybe you won't waver in your commitment to publish traditionally, but that doesn't mean you have to wait for only Penguin Random House to offer you a deal. Set your target, think on it daily,

hold it closely, and shift your approach when someone deto-
nates a hand grenade in your basket.

Like me, you've already embarked on an uncommon journey. Otherwise you wouldn't be reading this book. If you
mean to see the journey through you're going to need to cultivate an uncommon mindset.

Some will call you a fool for putting all your eggs in one
basket, but merely having the audacity to be a novelist is an
admission you'll have to go all-in. You can't do this professionally without giving it your whole heart, and if you don't
want to do this professionally why are you reading this book?

HARD AND CHALLENGING ARE NOT THE SAME

Challenging and hard overlap in areas, but diverge in others.
Pushing a car up a hill is hard work by anyone's definition,
but difficult by none. Making phone calls eight hours a day is
hard, and challenging. Figuring out how to make someone
smile…that's another challenge entirely.

Somewhere in that process you're going to want to quit.
It's okay if you decide the effort is too great, that the enjoyment is too little, but if you do feel that way, accept responsibility. I encourage you to. There's little benefit in self-
deception.

After about a year working at Second Nature, I was given
an opportunity to work on an oil rig. The company was called
Rocky Mountain Drilling, and I was going to be assigned as a
drill hand to a former coworker of mine from Second Nature.

The work was physical and the weather wild. Some shifts
would see me wielding a pry bar on a metal auger for twelve
hours, relentlessly. Those were the days when the drill hit
packed, wet clay. It was hard work, and often challenging too,
on account of the elements. Even in subzero temperatures,
you had to stand out in the cold, ready to work.

Some days, the drilling was light and the dirt crumbled with ease. But just because there was less for me to do cleaning out the auger did not mean I was allowed to relax. In the oil fields, the culture is busy-work-regardless, so on those days I might get a rag from the cab of the truck and clean the seats or arrange paperwork. Build a dirt mound. Anything to stay occupied.

If you were caught standing around you might be told to pack your crap and go home. There was no tolerance for "taking it easy."

Since I'd previously worked at Second Nature a week on and a week off, I had never chosen to rent an apartment. Instead, I opted to live out of my Chevy Blazer. Though my situation changed working for Rocky Mountain Drilling, I continued living out of my car, saving the rent money.

Whenever I had a day or two off work I'd travel wherever I wanted and spend without regard because I made good money and had no bills.

Several months into the job my stepbrother called me and asked if I knew any companies hiring. I'd befriended a rig hand at another company so I did a little poking around and helped my brother get work.

Two weeks after he arrived my brother found me before a shift and let me know he was quitting. Living out of his car was too challenging. He didn't mind the labor but found the changing environment taxing to his sleep, and if he had a day off he didn't know how to fend off boredom.

While I know he and I operated somewhat from personal preferences, there's a caution and a lesson from the oil fields for all of us who want to cultivate the seven-figure mindset toward our novels. Anyone can do hard work. It keeps you occupied, your mind off dissatisfaction, confusion, sadness or depression.

Those who choose to challenge themselves will be met with a host of obstacles. I no more enjoyed the cramped unpredictable climate of living out of my car than my brother did, but I embraced a vision my brother lacked.

The freedom to travel and spend money like an idiot illuminated a core part of my identity as an adventurer. For that reason, my threshold for discomfort was much greater.

As writers, this applies to all of us when we begin seeking readers. It is the challenge we need to be most clear-eyed toward.

If writing novels is the thing you most desire in life and having readers for those novels is an identity-level concern, you must develop a tenacity toward the challenge of finding readers.

The challenge most writers face is in their "I statements". Ask most writers and you'll find they say, "I'm not a marketer." Saying it makes it true. If you refuse to be defeated, you need to adopt a radical mindset toward this challenge. It'll require you to adapt your identity.

And I know, when I worked in the oil fields, I didn't have to change my identity. That part of me came as naturally as waking with this handsome face each morning. But you've come this far with me now so surely you remember how I once believed a great book would be all I needed and that I was not a marketer.

Faced with an ultimatum, I chose to change my identity, and you can too.

HARD WORK AS AN IDENTITY

A friend of mine and I frequently discuss hard work. Give him a shovel or a rake, and he'll outwork every person in the garden, but ask him to approach a stranger and request a loan and he'll run screaming.

To this day, I would love to operate a vacant land-buying and -selling business. But with all my energy focused on writing and producing a podcast I don't yet have the brain space to do both so I've approached my friend about spear-heading the business.

He would rather work at the local grocery to make money then spend his time learning to buy and sell vacant land. He feels like playing around with loans and debt and leverage is the gambler's road to lazy town. Hard work, he says, purifies the soul.

From his identity he creates his worldview. That world-view informs everything he does. He has a positive self-image if he knows he put in a hard day's work. He worries about his body deteriorating as he ages because if it does he won't be able to work as hard.

He looks forward to vacations as a just reward to relax after a long six months of hard work. He enjoys watching baseball at night and drinking beer because it's an escape from the hard work.

Nothing makes him feel more useful than if someone asks him to help tile a floor. He'd rather mow a lawn than sit on the porch and watch a sunset.

My friend has other identities as well, as we all do. He values being a good father. He values being a loving husband. He has built his entire life around these identities and what-ever he does or refuses to do, the choices arise from one of his identities.

THE POWER OF IDENTITY

You may consider compassion a core element of your identity. If you do, you'll tend to find yourself volunteering at soup kitchens, or helping homeless shelters.

It is without doubt the most effective way to accomplish anything to operate from a core identity.

The good news is, you're able to change your identity with thought and action. It's challenging work, but the rewards when you do may be the most lasting benefit this book has to offer.

Sometime in 2010 Ashley decided she wanted to quit Diet Coke. She'd been a Diet Coke fiend for most of her life, often drinking as many as sixteen cans a day.

Her love for Diet Coke was so sincere people identified her with it, and she identified herself with it, until the day she decided all of the artificial sweeteners could not be healthy for her.

She quit Diet Coke entirely. As you would imagine, she found it challenging for months, but as time passed she grew more distant from considering Diet Coke part of who she was. By the time we began dating she had formed a new identity as a person whose only and favorite beverage was coffee.

Some people go to great lengths to change their identities and need extreme support to do so. Alcoholics Anonymous is one such place that helps its members transform. (Ironically, though, AA also encourages its members to cling to and associate with their most damaging identity, that of their addiction.)

Our identities can and must change if we mean to be full-time, wealthy, influential novelists.

The purpose of the seven-figure marketing mindset is to help you embrace a new identity. If you want to be a full-time novelist you have to accept you are a marketer and begin behaving as one today.

You will encounter setbacks. You will feel tired. You will be embarrassed, angry, and disillusioned at times. But if you embrace your identity as a marketer you will see your tenacity in the face of hardships skyrocket.

IS IT REALLY AN IDENTITY IF IT CAN CHANGE?

Identities can and do change. You were born an infant, grew into a toddler, matured into a child, then a teen, and an adult. Eventually you'll qualify for senior discounts. Once you were a student, then you became an employee. Now you are a writer, husband, wife, father, mother, wealthy, poor. You choose the majority of your identities.

Some of our identities keep us down. Consider any time you say "I am not..." Often that phrase is a self-limiting governor keeping you from something, and a major aspect of the seven-figure mindset is protecting ourselves from harming our future by reinforcing destructive identities.

Guarding against regression is a daily effort. For me, positive thinking comes hard so I find I have to pump external affirmations into my ears, and through my eyes, hours every day. And as soon as I back away from affirmations negative thinking and destructive behavior is close at hand.

Nowhere is it more evident than my diet. Perhaps you are like me and have a constant battle with your waistline. My identity is fluid as my weight fluctuates on the scale.

One moment I'm skinny and healthy, the next I'm fat and lazy. Notice, in both cases, I wrote "I am". not "my body is". That's what happens with identity-level topics. It can motivate and make easy behaviors we want to cultivate, or it can stunt and hinder growth.

We want to use our identities as superfood to help us through hardships. Taking in external motivation is powerful, and there are even small self-talk behaviors that can produce major thought process changes.

Try this: pay attention to the ways you use the word "am". Every time you use the word "am" to enforce an undesired identity, replace the word with an external phrase instead. For example, change "I *am* hungry" to "*My stomach feels* hungry."

You'll be surprised how much less power the latter statement has over your thinking than the former phrase.

Try it the other way around too. If you catch yourself saying, "I have to market my book," change it to, "I *am* a book marketer." I get it. It might feel like semantics to you today, but the cumulative impact of daily speaking our identities over time has massive impacts on how we perceive ourselves.

Try this right now: it may feel like woo woo, but it helps. Tell someone you are a marketer. Pick up the phone if there's no one nearby. Doing so accelerates the transformation. (Though, don't be fooled into believing you change alone. Books like this, motivators like Lewis Howes and Ed Mylett, physical trainers, they all have a huge impact on our success.)

My grandmother's father was a lifelong cigarette smoker. Unlike me, he never wanted to quit. At the age of sixty-five he went for a physical and the doctor told him if he didn't quit smoking he'd be dead in six months.

Entrenched in his identity as a smoker, my great grandfather told the doctor he'd be dead in six months because smoking was one of life's only pleasures. True to the prophecy, my great grandfather died six months later. This story is, understandably, a legend in my family, and one with a sad outcome.

It also powerfully illustrates what we are able to do when we bind ourselves to an identity.

Are you a marketer?

BUSYNESS AS A DISTRACTION FROM AN IDENTITY CRISIS

In the spring of 2021, I stumbled into an uncommon kind of busyness. I was working at the direct mail marketing company.

I knew I wasn't interested in putting forth the creative energy to wring out the little extra money I could earn, but I also struggled with feeling unethical about how little meaningful work I did for the company.

I made myself incredibly busy writing and sending emails to potential clients during that period so I didn't have to get in my car, drive to a restaurant, get out of the car, go inside, and deliver my pitch.

I behaved like a coward, and I regret that. It did teach me a lesson though and one I have brought into my life operating my own small business. It's a mindset that if you cultivate can help you hone your identities rather than dulling them.

Every time you notice yourself feeling busier than ever, pause what you're doing and evaluate the quality of your actions. Is the activity producing money, brand growth, or giving others value? If not, you'll find something in your process you're doing specifically to distract yourself from something challenging you're afraid to confront. Something that if you do confront has the ability to transform your life.

BURNOUT AS PROOF YOU HAVE LOST YOUR IDENTITY

A sure and easy sign fear is controlling you is burnout.

We've been taught burnout is a result of working too hard or too much. That's simply false. Burnout happens when we know what we're doing isn't moving us where we need to go, but we either have no idea how to get there or the sacrifices we have to make seem too great.

In either scenario, fear begins to drive distracting activity so we can divert ourselves from something we prefer to hide from. The vast expense of energy to avoid a problem leads to the burnout we feel.

If you've ever vacationed because you felt burnt out and hoped to feel refreshed but returned more fatigued than when you left, you understand why burnout isn't an overwork problem.

You're probably even familiar with the common saying "I

need a vacation from my vacation." If you feel that way, it's proof you're avoiding a challenging truth. Rather than a vacation, the solution to burnout is to stop all busyness, stop all work, and take inventory of the situation you find yourself in.

For us novelists the issue may look like too few copies of our book sold. Perhaps our newsletter is growing too slowly or the people on the list have too low of an open rate. Maybe your conversion rate on clicks when they do open a newsletter is too meager.

You may feel at a loss for how to grow your TikTok or Instagram or Twitter, but instead of asking for help you tweet more or you create more Instagram or TikTok videos without asking yourself why the content isn't connecting in the first place.

Still, when all the busyness in the world doesn't fix the problem, it doesn't stop you from being busier and busier until finally you're cooked and disillusioned and seeking that vacation that won't relax you.

Your solution to solve any given problem will be different than mine, but if you have the mindset to spot the problem you are sure to progress faster, with less friction, and further.

It is the mindset here that matters so much. Cultivate the mindset of an observer. Dig into statistics. Ask yourself which activities produce noticeable results. Dissect those activities. Something you did was unique from your other efforts. Once you pinpoint the success and know how to go where you're going again, your burnout will dissolve like fog at noon.

DIET, EFFICIENCY AND MINDSET

Have you ever needed to lose some weight, started a diet and seen pounds melt off only to run into a holiday? If so, you know what it feels like to upset the routine.

This matters because often, when we've found a successful rhythm it can be both frightening and dangerous to change our approach. If you were finding success counting calories and someone told you fasting was more effective, you'd have a decision to evaluate.

Now, I'm not a doctor, and as such, this is not medical advice. Seek a health professional if you want qualified dietary counsel. That being said, there is ample proof time-restricted-feeding has metabolic advantages beyond calorie counting.

These benefits include increased insulin sensitivity, reduced blood pressure, fat loss (specifically visceral fat which is the dangerous fat surrounding your vital organs), cellular repair, brain and cognitive protection, anti-aging and more.

All of these benefits increase in effectiveness as time-restricted feeding (periods of total caloric restriction between twelve and twenty-four hours) moves into water fasting (periods greater than twenty-four hours.

By contrast, calorie counting causes the body to slow its metabolism. If you've ever calorie counted before, you know each pound you lose results in a lower calorie allowance. That's because the body responds to restriction by lowering its metabolic demands.

Ironically, total deprivation leads to a key metabolic shift: the body moves away from carbohydrate preference to fat preference, burning your body's fat storage for ketones which can be used to fuel every organ in the body. (The brain will always require a few carbohydrates to survive, but the body can use minimal lean tissues [proteins] to create carbohydrates needed for the brain.

If this is all seeming a little too sciency for you, hang with me for another moment.

When the body shifts to fat burning, and all of the above-mentioned processes deepen, the body's weight set-point will change. Its efficiency at burning carbs when carbs are reintroduced will improve, its efficiency at using nutrients will rise, and muscle repair and growth will speed.

In the simplest terms, using fasting for weight loss allows you to eat more when you are eating and maintain weight where calorie-counting slowly reduces what you can eat to maintain weight to unmanageable levels.

So you can lose weight by calorie counting, but at some point, the vast majority of dieters fail and cannot sustain the lifestyle. The body simply isn't made for a 900-calorie-a-day diet.

But, many people experience extreme challenges in the early phases if they try to switch from calorie-counting to fasting for health. If you've never gone 24-, 48- or 72-hours without food, it requires grit and determination.

That difficulty can lead to quitting diets all together, which many people who try to transition find happens, and if you make the transition from calorie restriction to fasting, you'll soon encounter a holiday that wants to bust your rhythm.

Miss a day, or start eating before your time-restricted window ends and you will find it can be tough to shift the mindset back toward fasting.

And all of this applies to marketing your writing because when you identify something about your process that needs to be better, you'll be faced with discomfort and challenge.

HOW EXERCISE REVEALS OUR MARKETING CREATIVITY MINDSET

At various times in my life I've been an enthusiastic runner. I enjoy distance more than sprints. Once I push past the first few miles a sort of meditative calmness takes over my breathing and my muscles stretch out.

Unfortunately, my body has never loved running as much as my mind. All too often I've had to transition to stationary biking or using an elliptical machine because my shins are weak and they get splints.

No matter how hard I try to run through the pain, I cannot overcome shin splints without resting my legs. The problem is, when I rest I weaken my legs, and so eventually the shin splints return the next time I run.

I tried everything from losing weight to barefoot running, but nothing prevented the injury until I discovered the Knees Over Toes Guy[17].

His videos exposed the flaw in how leg strengthening and protection had always been taught. Instead of doing our best to avoid getting our knees over our toes, the secret to preventing all manner of leg injuries was to become pliable and strong in that knees over toes range.

It's awfully tough to become great at something when we're working with faulty information. If the information you've been using all your life is wrong, it's no wonder the outcomes keep missing the target. The same is true for our marketing.

You've been told lies like "nepotism is bad," and "quality rises to the top" and "if you're true to yourself that's all that matters."

The truth is, if you learn to benefit from nepotism, you gain a huge advantage. If you accept marketing helps us rise to the top you embrace the work in more meaningful ways. And if you confront the truth that no one cares how authentic you are until they see why your authenticity matters to them, you have an opportunity to launch the most lucrative and productive times of your life.

Flip expectations on their head, get ready to go all out, increase intensity when others are complaining about the scourge nepotism is on the face of the earth, and you'll emerge with some very uncommon rewards.

DISCOMFORT IS A FEATURE OF THE FUTURE

When you go all out, you're going to experience great discomfort. Don't confuse discomfort for injury. Shin splints are a problem, and you can't beat them by pushing through, but you can beat them by changing how you work.

When you strengthen your knees in all ranges of motion, you won't get shin splints no matter how often you run, but you have to learn how to run correctly first.

Once you have learned to run correctly, you'll still feel discomfort as you push yourself to new levels of achievement. Faster and further is going to require pain.

You know you are approaching a seven-figure marketing mindset when you welcome pain as a sign you're pursuing something worth achieving, and this is one area where it's critical you adapt the mindset of collaboration, because if you try to pursue excellence alone you may struggle to differentiate injury and discomfort.

Invite others on a similar journey to look into your efforts. Others have the ability to see where our form is either correct and building strength, or faulty and leading to injury.

You might be asking yourself, "What do injury and book marketing have to do with each other"?

It's easy to sell a book—yes, I said it's easy to sell a book—but it's difficult to win a reader. If you knock on enough doors you'll sell a book. If the book you sell doesn't deliver the promise you told the buyer it would, they will not continue to read your work. You get one chance.

Misrepresenting what you wrote is the same as injuring yourself during exercise.

You know me well enough now to know my sense of morality is a little off-north, but if there's one area where I don't mince words or fudge definitions, it's in the purpose of my books.

I want to be known as the person with the highest degree

of integrity regarding my books. I will not sell a book just to sell a book, and you shouldn't either.

Don't apologize for your work, and don't minimalize what you're attempting to achieve. Perhaps you write steamy sex scenes. Advertise that. Don't hide it. Maybe you write horror. Don't try to make less of the gruesome details. Let them shine.

It's easy to allow others to define who we are for us, but if we want to be successful to an extreme degree we have to own who we are and what we write. Writing who we are is the equivalent of the Knees Over Toes Guy showing us how to make our knees invulnerable to everyday stresses.

PHYSICAL BEHAVIORS THAT IMPROVE YOUR MINDSET

You've probably heard the phrase "get comfortable being uncomfortable," but of all the misleading phrases, this one might be in the top three most damaging.

You aren't ever going to be comfortable with discomfort, but you can learn to crave it, to thrive because of it, and to embrace it. There are, in fact, a handful of behaviors you can practice to strengthen your tolerance and resolve in the face of discomfort.

Action creates mindset. If you want to be the kind of writer who resists the urge to quit when you experience discomfort around marketing, try one of these three behaviors. Be warned, they improve resolve because they are, in themselves, uncomfortable behaviors.

Not all discomfort is created equal though. Running does not improve your resolve to keep running any more than dieting improves your resolve to diet.

However, a bracing, five-minute, cold shower will improve your resolve to keep running or dieting. Again, I'm not a physician. Be sure you're healthy enough if you want to try cold showers.

And if cold doesn't seem like your gig, try tummo breathing. The combination of hyperventilation and breath holding creates powerful physiological changes that have proven benefits to stress and anxiety management: the very tools you need to endure discomfort in other areas of your life—like marketing.

If you don't want to do cold showers, and breath holding sounds nightmarish you might remember our door-to-door bookselling exercise. Turns out, talking to strangers is proven to improve our discomfort tolerance. The key here is to talk to strangers in a safe, sober setting. Alcohol mediated intimacy negates the benefits. It's possible I'm writing to myself here.

If you want extra credit, and you're healthy enough, try all three!

CHAPTER
SEVEN

LOOSE ENDS - RAPID FIRE ROUND

1. Retirement Planning

If our minds are the castle, we're now deep into a battering ram offensive. Why not level the gates? Another analogy to help you with your journey toward a seven-figure marketing mindset can be found in retirement planning.

You've likely been told you should invest in a 401k or an IRA for your retirement. Doing this, you'll see that account grow over the life of your career.

However, the moment you invest in the fund, you lock the dollar away until you reach age 65. No matter what happens, you've separated yourself from that dollar.

Would you write a book so you could sell it and enjoy the earnings in thirty-years? Of course you wouldn't! We want access to that money immediately. Some of it we might live on, other bits we might reinvest in advertising, still more we might use to start another book.

So who convinced us a 401k is a beneficial behavior?

Good is the enemy of better.

2. There's No Such Thing as Perfect but There Is Better

Perhaps you've heard the saying, "Perfect is the enemy of good."

The saying is true, but it is also true that "Good is the enemy of better."

How do you know when perfectionism is hindering action, and how do you know when the reverse is happening, good enough is hindering innovation?

It's better to act than to think. Any action is better than no action. But if you find you feel bored or burnt out, chances are, you're involved in low-quality action. Change the behavior and you'll be surprised how much better your results will be.

3. Some Things You Do Are A Product of Inaction

It's easy to know if you suffer from "perfectionism" because you find yourself editing, tweaking, correcting, and redrafting but never sending your product into the world. If there's any better reason to hire an editor than this, I can't think of one. How many more books might you have sold if you'd sped the editing and got your work out there?

If you think you're saving money by self-editing, your real problem is with low expectations. You'd not mind spending the cash on an editor if you believed your book could sell enough copies to pay for the expense.

. . .

4. Radical Action Is the <u>ONLY</u> Choice

Radical action produces radical mindset shifts. Look at the actions you're taking today toward marketing your book. Identify the one that produces the least results. Hire someone to take that action from you and add more into your flow.

If that action you hired out is so low value you can't justify paying for it, you need to stop doing it all together. Now is the time to cut that action.

Likely, the lowest value action is one you're still in charge of, because as we've already identified, we tend to struggle with spending money on our marketing so we naturally only part with that money for activities we believe provide return. The point here, though, is to help us understand the difference between what we give and what we get.

Immediately stop doing the lowest value action you've been doing. You're going to avoid that action for one week and evaluate gains and losses in marketing. If you can't see a dip in book sales, the action was a time-waster and now you are more efficient.

If you did notice a drop in book sales, resume the action and quit another low-value action.

5. Replace Low-Value Action With High-Value Action

Once a week, I was using SocialDog—remember that amazing Twitter automation tool that tracks followers, and many other statistics—I was using it to unfollow those who don't follow me back.

While I'm sure we all hate the optics of social media, there is value in improving our follow ratios. The more followers we have and the fewer people we follow, the more successful we are perceived to be.

But how high-value do you think it was for me to mindlessly click on profile after profile and unfollow those people? A great candidate for a VA to help me with a few hours a month. The action needs to be done, but I could do something far higher-leverage than that.

Other low-value actions I do that you might relate to include proofreading my previous day's writing, audio editing podcast episodes, organizing and replying to incoming emails, and cleaning my office or work spaces.

Any or all of those actions should be replaced with higher-value actions like researching blogs, podcasts, and local media opportunities. Build relationships with the people in those areas and write guest blogs, pitch guest appearances on the podcasts and find ways to meet and interact with your local media personnel.

All of those actions will require a nuance you can't hire out, and a personal touch only you possess. When you actively move away from the low- to the high-value actions, your mindset transforms and you begin to see numerous other actions you can move away from. You also gain an eye for high-leverage behaviors.

PROOF OF GROWTH

If, as you've been progressing through this book, you've acted when challenged to act, and embraced the discomfort, you'll have seen an increase in book sales, an increase in influence, and a growth of your platform.

We've reached the final pages. You'll be going out into the world alone. You have given much asked for little. It's time for another ask, but now you're asking for a favor.

Asking for a favor is a great challenge for many authors.

You feel as though you are transitioning away from relationship into "sales mode" and that causes you discomfort.

The more impactful mindset is to review what you have given. They have been enriched by your story. You gave them excitement, encouragement, thrill, and delight.

You know your book is valuable, but you seem to think asking your audience to engage with you in any way that benefits you is bad.

Consider this: if your favorite author today tweeted a call for help, asking her followers to retweet something, would you feel put out or would you jump at the opportunity to help?

Perhaps the strangest truth about that moment is, you would feel even closer to the author because you helped her when she needed something.

This is a strange truth about building relationships. When we ask others for a favor and they help us, we see an immediate strengthening of the bond. They feel closer to us. You'd assume the opposite, that they'd feel put off, but they don't.

One warning is required here, though. You have to only ask for high-value favors such as "Buy my book" or "Retweet this important announcement" (the announcement has to be high value!) or "Rate or review my book on a specific platform." or "Tell a friend / give someone a copy of my book."

These actions may seem like huge requests. You're asking people to open their wallet, to spend their time to improve your outlook. But if you can show the value and it's obvious what people gain, those who help now feel like part of your team, and that togetherness brings them closer in.

Reward your fans. When someone helps you, let them know how much it means to you. This may seem like an obvious action, but you will find when you have people promoting your work that in a sense, you have an urge to keep distance between yourself and the person.

We feel that engaging with the fan somehow reduces our

prestige. You might not use that word, but you'll recognize the hesitance to interact directly after someone buys or reviews our work.

Overcome that resistance and instead take an opportunity to gush about how great they are. By doing that you create a mindset of gratitude and reinforce the truth that your fans and audience enable you to do what you love to do.

If you've read this book as it's meant to be consumed, you've been driving at radical marketing mindset shifts and you're brimming with new ideas on how to put your book in new readers' hands. What is the biggest change you've seen in your mindset? Write it down. Reflect on it.

What is the biggest change you still need to see to have the kind of book sales you've always dreamed of? Write it down. Let's create a plan.

It's time to act. Go out there and sell that book. Oh, and if you found value in The Seven-Figure Marketing Mindset For Novelists, buy a copy for a friend; rate and review it on Goodreads and Amazon; tweet about it. And I thank you!

END NOTES

Social Dog

2

Xero Shoes

3

THE LAST KEEPER by JV HILLIARD
4

GREETINGS FROM BELOW *by David Phillip Mullins*

5

TO ASSUME A PLEASING SHAPE *by Joseph Salvatore*

6

FAIRY TALE by Stephen King

7

THE NATURAL by Bernard Malamud

8

William Shakespeare's Complete Works

9

M TRAIN by Patti Smith

10

2666 by Roberto Bolano

11

VOICES FROM THE MOON by Andre Dubus

12

INFINITE JEST by David Foster Wallace

13

JESUS' SON by Denis Johnson

14

BE OBSESSED OR BE AVERAGE by Grant Cardone

15

THIS IS MARKETING by Seth Godin

16

REACH by Becky Robinson

17

Knees Over Toes Guy - Ben Patrick

FINAL NOTES

CHAPTER 4

1. According to College Gazette

CHAPTER 6

1. Note that the average literary journal publishes roughly 60 stories/poems/essays/interviews per issue; assume that moms buy their children's work, and accept that most journals are moving about fifteen to ninety copies of each print run. If that doesn't sound perfectly miserable to you, I'm not sure what you could endure, because a passion project that no one is passionate about is a waste of time at the very least...